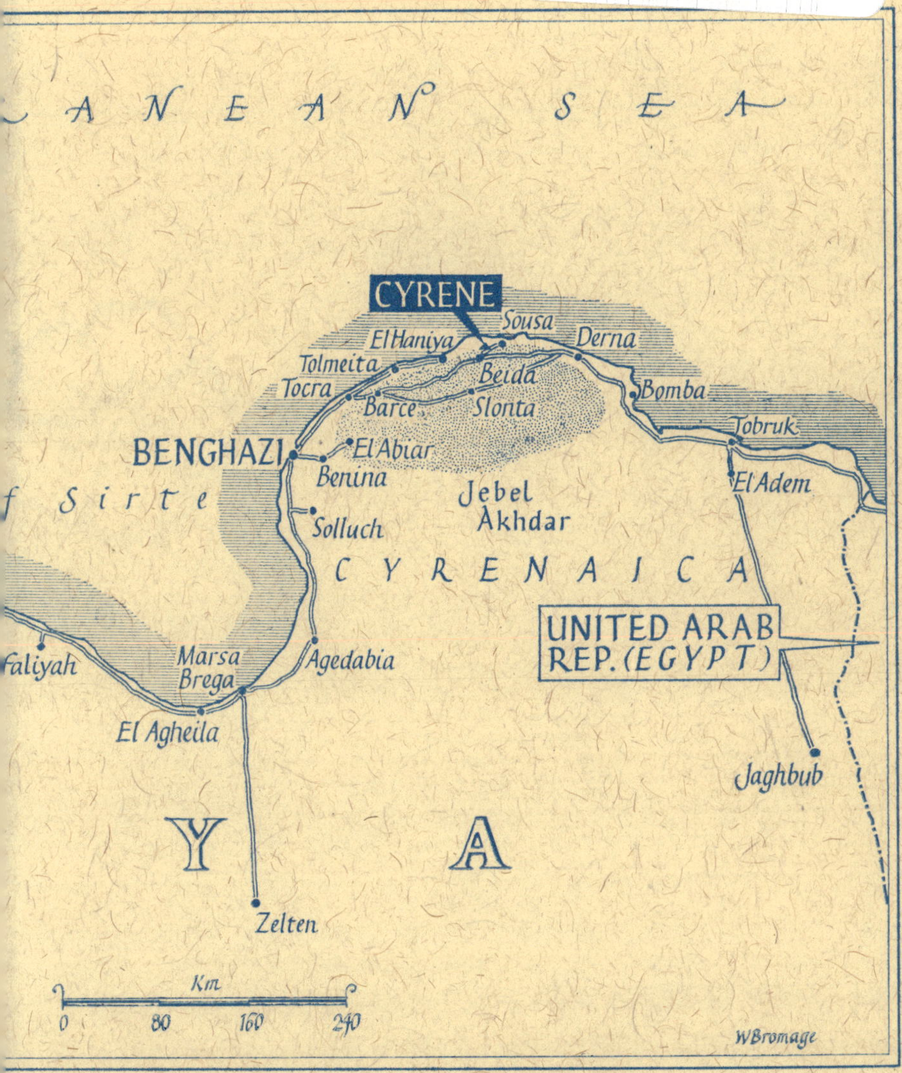
ANEAN SEA
CYRENE
Sousa
El Haniya
Derna
Tolmeita
Beida
Tocra
Bomba
Barce
Slonta
Tobruk
BENGHAZI
El Abiar
Benina
El Adem
Jebel
Akhdar
f Sirte
Solluch
CYRENAICA
UNITED ARAB
REP. (EGYPT)
faliyah
Marsa
Brega
Agedabia
El Agheila
Jaghbub
Y
A
Zelten
Km
0
80
160
240
W Bromage

The Deserts of Hesperides

The Deserts of
HESPERIDES

An Experience of Libya * by
ANTHONY THWAITE

SECKER & WARBURG · LONDON

SBN 436 53950 0

First published in England 1969 by
Martin Secker & Warburg Limited
14 Carlisle Street London W1

Printed in Great Britain by
Cox & Wyman Limited
London, Fakenham and Reading

Contents

Contents

Illustrations

For my parents, Alice and Hartley Thwaite

Preface

THIS book is a record of my life in and reactions to Libya during the two periods I have lived there: first as a British army conscript in Tripolitania from June 1950 to July 1951, then as a university teacher in Cyrenaica from September 1965 to July 1967. That there is a connection between the two – that my second stay was the result of my first – quickly becomes apparent. To revisit a Land of Lost Content is supposed to be a mistake, and I dare say it generally is. One thinks of those public school Captains of Games who, on leaving university, tunnel back as quickly as possible into the golden world of youth by returning to those same public schools as masters, and spend the rest of their lives training up new Captains of Games. But my return to Libya was different, partly because at thirty-five I was quite aware of the illusions of twenty, and partly because I came not to Tripolitania, the western province of the country, but to Cyrenaica in the east, which I had never seen before. And in Benghazi I settled down with my family and became part of a Libyan institution, rather than being a single soldier forced by circumstance on to the periphery of Libyan life.

No one has yet written a wholly satisfactory book about Libya: the journals of nineteenth-century and later desert travellers, war memoirs, archaeological monographs, economic and sociological surveys, accounts such as Gwyn Williams's *Green Mountain* and Agnes Newton Keith's *Children of Allah* – many of these give attractive and interesting glimpses but all are in some way narrow and partial. I can't suppose that my own account is any less so, but I hope that at any rate it gives some sense of the feel of this huge and still little-known country, so close to Europe and yet so remote. If there are more ruins than oil-rigs in the book, that is a matter of my own antiquarian tastes; if there seem to be more ruins than *people*, I have little to fall back on but that remark of Rose Macaulay's that she often found ruins more interesting than people. Ignorance dictates my sub-title: this book is an experience, a personal one, and does not set out to be authoritative and definitive.

Among the many people who have helped me to write it, through their advice (which I haven't always taken), their conversation, or their company on journeys, I must mention particularly Pablo Foster, the late Richard Goodchild, Stephen Levinson, Andrew Murray and Peter Wakefield among the Englishmen; among Libyans, so many have helped that I cannot list all their names, and in any case such listing might be an embarrassment to them, implying concurrence with what I have to say. I alone am responsible for any errors of fact or interpretation. It is customary for authors to thank their wives: in this case all I can say is that I can never be sufficiently grateful to mine for the way in which she not only agreed but encouraged me to uproot ourselves – all six of us, including a five-month-old baby – for two years to go to a country which to her, in 1965, was just one of my frequently rehearsed daydreams. That our stay ended with the fury and bitterness of the June 1967 war is our only regret about the whole enterprise.

Anthony Thwaite

In the Gardens of Hesperides
The dragon and his nymphs patrol
The rich fruits of the underworld –
Ripe swollen figs hang from the trees,
The date-palm and the prickly pear,
The olive and the orchid thrive,
And in that harvest-freighted air
The desert dies upon the breeze.

But legends shift localities
As men desire them to, and now
Scylax and Ptolemy would not see
In local oddities like these
Strangeness at all. Look at the sand:
Far to the south black gold wells up
Out of a dry and fruitless land,
The Deserts of Hesperides.

1 Leptis Discovered

IN the grounds of Windsor Great Park, at Virginia Water, some marble columns and monumental masonry lie about with the carefully disposed inconsequentiality of some late eighteenth- or early nineteenth-century folly. It is something of a shock to see on one of them the resonant carved words 'Africa! Africa!', and to realize that these are authentic pieces of Roman Libya. They seem incongruous exotica in this pastoral landscape. Certainly they are far from home.

What happened was that in 1817 Commander W. H. Smyth, R. N., a serving officer with antiquarian tastes rare among serving officers today, managed to persuade his chief on Malta to let him go with Lord Exmouth's expedition along the north African coast. Smyth even got a grant from the British government to help him in his plundering researches. Among the sites he attempted to scavenge was Leptis Magna, eighty miles east of Tripoli, a Roman coastal city which at that time was almost completely lost under sand dunes, with little indication on the surface of what lay underneath. But Smyth's excavations were neither gratifying nor very productive. 'The destruction is complete,' he recorded gloomily, and abandoned the whole unscientific effort. As it turns out, he had had bad luck: he happened to choose for his main dig the middle of the site of the Severan Forum, the one place in Leptis which had been almost totally destroyed, though its scattered parts have now been splendidly reassembled. But he salvaged enough columns and carvings to send back to the Prince Regent, at whose wish, presumably, they were erected in tasteful desuetude at Virginia Water.

Smyth was one of the earliest European travellers to venture into Libya in modern times. One hundred and forty-three years later, on my twentieth birthday, I followed him, with several hundred other assorted military. I was Acting (Paid) Sergeant, R.A.E.C., not long out of school, eager for ruins and forbidden fruit, probably in that order. The troopship *Halladale* docked at Tripoli on June 23rd, 1950: and there to meet me was my friend

❋ 2

Harry Scammell, whom I had got to know at the R.A.E.C. training school in Bodmin. He was a geologist, a palaeobotanist, employed at the British Museum in civilian life and scholarly about many topics. It was Harry who had encouraged me to try to get a posting to Libya, and not only to Libya but specifically to the garrison at Homs, where he had been stationed for some months and which was only a mile from Leptis Magna; Harry had written me ecstatic letters about wine and sun and sea and ruins.

For once, the army acted as one would have wished. Others fared less well: back at Bodmin, at that odd training school, I had heard gloomily of Heathering, who had sought adventure in Malaya but who had inexplicably been sent to Colchester, and of Yates, who had asked for a home-posting to Nottingham because of his invalid mother but who was banished to Hong Kong. What was the point of listing preferences if this sort of thing happened? But I wrote down '6th Field Regt., R.A., Homs, Tripolitania', and in due course heard that that was precisely where I was going.

Tripoli in June was hot and blindingly sunny. I can remember little about those first days except the dust and heat of the transit camp on the Sabratha road just outside Tripoli, and some experimental drinking evenings with Harry in the Italian restaurants along the Corso Vittorio Emmanuele. Libya was still under the British Military Administration, though due for independence not later than January 1st, 1952, and there were many superficial signs of the old *status quo*: the Italian street names, the anomalous currency (*lire*, but Military Administration Lire, or MAL as it was known), the streets themselves full of Italian shops and Italians. If one went through the archway by the Castello which led to the old city, one was confronted with OUT OF BOUNDS signs on every alley corner. The Italian Bishop of Tripoli had from the pulpit officially discouraged fraternization between British troops and Italians. The Arabs themselves, who were soon to inherit this country, followed their traditionally menial occupations, not markedly better off, it seemed, under the British than under the Italians. There was, in those first days of mine, something oppressive or depressed about Tripoli, and I was eager to get out of the transit camp and off to Homs.

✳ 3

This happened after about a week. A 15-cwt. truck collected me and my kit-bag, and we drove the eighty miles eastward, much of it through fertile country with olives, oranges and vines. At that time Tripoli was surrounded by British garrisons, all of them housed in ex-Italian barracks. These large pink and yellow blocks still quite clearly bore the remains of that Fascist penchant for slapping up grandiose slogans: DUCE or VV IL DUCE or VV IL RE, or CREDERE OBBEDIRE COMBATTERE, or – more interestingly – passages from d'Annunzio's poems, full of references to Roman eagles and Roman legions. I realized later, during my 1965-7 stay in Libya, one reason why most Libyans take no interest in the Roman monuments: to them, they are just another manifestation of Fascism – as Graziani never ceased to remind his troops, 'Remember that you are Italians, Romans, and remember that your forebears were once in this country.'

Homs was in 1950, and still is, a small coastal town with a population of a few thousand. The ex-Blackshirt barracks dominate the town to the east. Here the artillery regiment to which I had been posted was quartered. My duties were vague. Harry and I were supposed to work under the direction of an R.A.E.C. warrant officer, Bill Humphreys, but, as in most army units, education was not very seriously catered for. If Saturday morning was set aside, as it occasionally was, for so-called Interior Economy (cleaning up the camp area, picking up fag ends, sweeping the barrack square), we might find ourselves with a class or so. Occasionally there were maniacal bursts of activity when it was decided that some of the regular Other Ranks would have to take an examination. But on the whole Bill Humphreys got on with running the local branch of the Elks (a sub-masonic cult), and Harry and I blew the sand off the office files in the morning and set off for Leptis in the afternoon. I can't pretend that I was fully stretched, in any Reithian sense, at Homs.

From the large window of the room I shared with Harry, we looked over the small pink Catholic church, the gleaming white mosque with its minaret from which the *muezzin* pitched his high nasal cry at four o'clock every morning and then four more times during the day and night, the married quarters for the British army families (small bungalows, originally built for Italian dependents), the harbour buildings and the quay, and then the wide blue stretch of the Mediterranean, fringed with a gleaming white beach which runs for over two miles eastward, to Leptis and beyond. Immediately below our window was a butcher's shop, with festoons of guts and tripes swinging fly-blown in the breeze from the sea, and sometimes a camel's head sitting on the pavement, its long twisted tongue lolling out of its mouth. The smell from the shop and the bantering and donkey-braying from the market wafted up into the room, where we used to lie in the evening, often fuming with 'Oea' chemical beer (the Tripolitanian equivalent of the Egyptian 'Stella') or sickly draughts of rum and orange, a drink to which both of us had become attached at Bodmin but which – after a particularly extravagant bout towards the end of my time at Homs – I have never touched again. In the Sergeants' Mess the usual week-end pattern, generally avoided by us, the babies of the Mess, was for serious drinking to begin on Friday afternoon and to go on without interruption until Sunday night. The most flagrant example of this was when the pipe-band of the Cameron Highlanders arrived for a pointless semi-social occasion known as a 'Regimental week-end'; the band, including its pipe-major, were so incapably drunk as they attempted to march and countermarch on the Homs barrack square that they were ordered off and immediately whisked back to their quarters in Tripoli. The Homs Sergeants' Mess felt inordinately proud that they had reduced the aggressively tough and hard-drinking Scottish N.C.O.s to such a condition, while still remaining moderately on their feet themselves.

Apart from a cannery for tunny fish and a soap factory (both still functioning), there seemed to be little work in Homs. A great deal of time, for Arabs, Italians and British army alike, was spent in sitting about in the pavement cafés. There was one Italian-run restaurant, the *Venete*, where we ate steak, pasta and chicken very cheaply, augmented with huge portions of chips which the Italian waiters refused to modify, no matter how many times one urged them to deposit 'Una *morsella* di patata!' The old *signora* in charge presided over the place with a graciousness and dignity far beyond the deserts of her British clientele, most of whom grumbled, belched, argued truculently with the waiters, and occasionally vomited noisily over the tablecloths; for the wine was cheap too. When I returned sixteen years later, I was astonished to find the same *signora* there, looking no older, still inclined over her little bow-fronted desk at the back. The menu was now considerably more expensive and the customers almost exclusively Italian, for the British army had left Homs barracks and handed over to the Libyan army in 1963. But it turned out that the waiter (a Libyan) had been batman to the Regimental Sergeant-Major when I had been stationed in Homs, and had later joined the Libyan army for ten years, during which time he had been to Britain on a course. He consequently spoke English with a rich command of that vocabulary of contempt and dismissiveness which is the mark of the British soldier.

There is now a bleak but reasonably priced hotel in Homs, which – as long as one eats not there but at the *Venete* – is a good base for seeing Leptis. In front of it are the municipal gardens, a mathematically laid-out stretch of uncomfortable stone benches and wilting flower-beds, which one of my students who came from Homs proudly pointed out as the chief innovation in his home town. Between the gardens and the sea wooden beach-huts have been built, an addition to the place since I first knew it but not an attractive one, since most of them are already beginning to collapse. Altogether, there wasn't and isn't a great deal to detain one in Homs itself. It is towards Leptis that one looks from here.

There are two ways to Leptis from Homs: along the main road to the east, or along the beach. The road is quicker – fifteen or twenty minutes on foot – but the approach along the beach is more exciting. Already at Homs you can see the columns, honey-coloured and white, rising above the dunes on the shore, and the sand quite quickly begins to be littered with potsherds and fragments of masonry. Although the official entrance, where visitors sign the book and buy postcards, is by the roadside, there is nothing to stop you approaching the city from the eastern or western shore entries, completely unpatrolled then and only sporadically patrolled now. And despite the large fiercely-worded notice standing by the main entrance, which threatens punitive fines and even imprisonment for offences against the monuments or the carrying away of objects, one gets little impression of the almost excessive zeal common to the guardians of Greek,

✳ 6

Italian or Egyptian sites. Again, Leptis is one of the few major sites left in the Western world almost entirely untouched by organized parties of sightseers, professional guides and their polyglot harangues, and such intrusions as transistors and people cleaning their false teeth in Steradent behind the Corinthian columns.

But though the shore approach to Leptis has much to recommend it, most visitors will inevitably begin at the main entrance: and this has the advantage of showing dramatically the difference in level between ancient and modern. A flight of thirty steps leads down from the entrance path to the Roman road the Italian archaeologists called the 'Via Triunfale', across which stands the Arch of Septimius Severus. This has been under reconstruction for some time, and the elaborate marble sculpture from it, which during my first stay was ranged along the high ground to the south-east, where the winged victories and processional triumphal figures glittered in the open air, is now displayed more meaningfully but less evocatively in the Castle Museum in Tripoli. Still, the arch is there (a reconstructed model of it can be seen at the main entrance), and it is fitting that Septimius should be one's introduction to the city. For he was the man who substantially was responsible for the Leptis we see today. He was born there in A.D. 146, into a family which still spoke Punic, and to the end of his life he spoke Latin with his native accent. When he became Emperor in 193, after showing himself to be a brilliant military commander, it is said that he invited his sister to come from Leptis and visit him in Rome; but he soon sent her packing back to Leptis, for she publicly embarrassed him because she could speak hardly any Latin. The story shows how deeply a part of his background he was, and to understand Leptis (and Oea – ancient Tripoli – and Sabratha) one must understand its Punic background. Nothing of the original Phoenician settlement remains above ground, but excavation has shown that it lay on the promontory where the Roman lighthouse now stands, was of about the seventh century B.C., and that a Phoenician cemetery lay under the early Roman theatre – itself a gift to the city by a local man of Phoenician descent, Annobal Rufus, whose generosity is commemorated there in inscriptions written in both Latin and a late form of Punic. It was this theatre that Montgomery (with fine

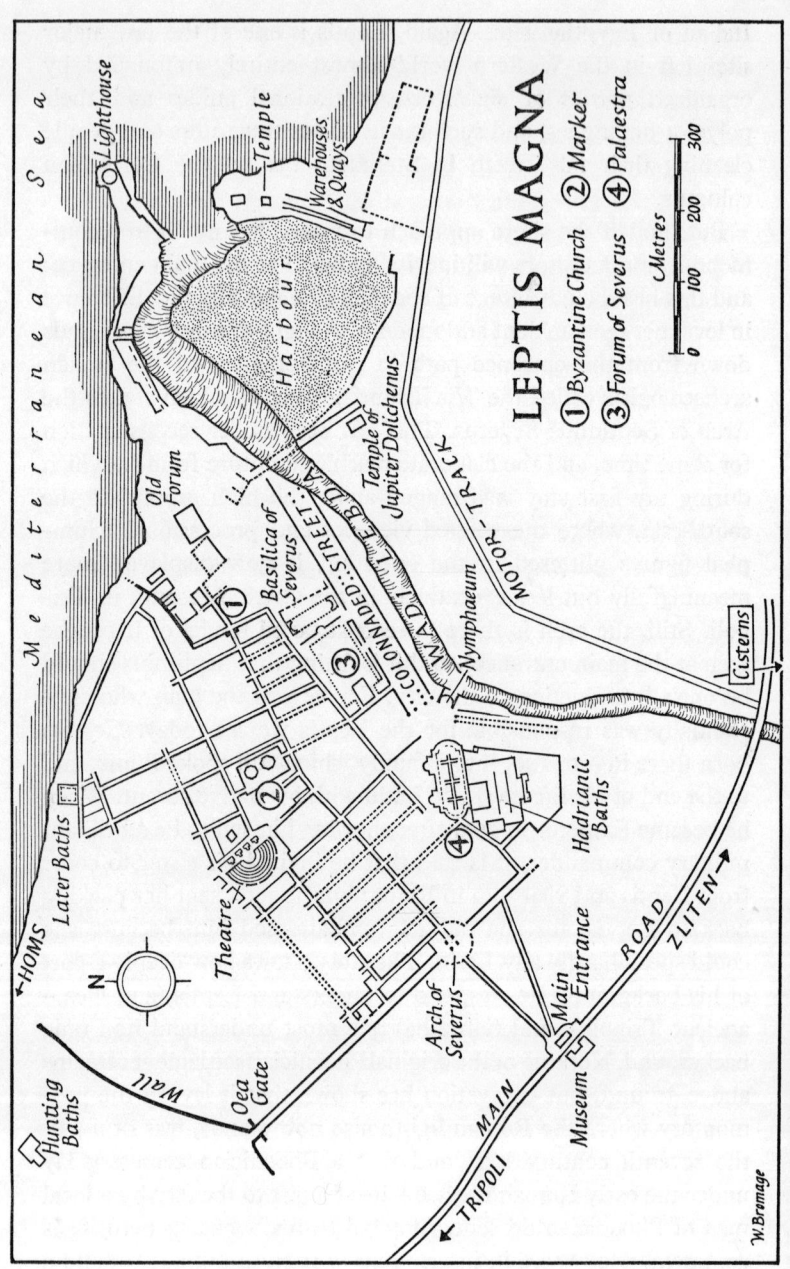

LEPTIS MAGNA

① Byzantine Church ② Market
③ Forum of Severus ④ Palaestra

Metres

0 100 200 300

Mediterranean Sea

Lighthouse

Temple

Warehouses & Quays

Harbour

Old Forum

Temple of Jupiter Dolichenus

Basilica of Severus

COLONNADED STREET

WADI LEBDA

Nymphaeum

MOTOR TRACK

Cisterns

Later Baths

←HOMS

N

Theatre

Hadrianic Baths

Wall

Oea Gate

Arch of Severus

Main Entrance

Museum

MAIN

ROAD

ZLITEN→

←TRIPOLI

Hunting Baths

W. Bramage

※ 8

histrionic imagination) chose as his site for a final pep-talk to his troops on the last push towards Tripoli in early 1943.

With the exception of this theatre and the Hadrianic Baths, the most sumptuous of the building at Leptis was done in the time of Septimius Severus: the Severan Arch, the Colonnaded Street, the Nymphaeum (a huge decorative fountain), the artificial harbour, and, most spectacularly, the Severan Forum and Basilica. When these had been built, Leptis reached the height of its development and the peak of its population – something over 80,000. The town began, not with brick but with the local building stone, a type of limestone from the Jebel Nefusa which was soft and porous and weathered very badly: Septimius turned it into a city of marble – in facings and in columns – which was quarried all over the Roman Empire and brought to Leptis, often ready cut and shaped for its destined places. There was green porphyry, grey granite and pentelic marble from the mainland of Greece, green breccia and red porphyry from Egypt, green cipollino from the island of Euboea, giallo antico from Numidia, synnadicum from Phrygia. The complexity and expense of all this can be judged from the fact that Roman cargo-ships were so small that probably only one or two columns of the size found at Leptis could be carried in one journey. Many of the columns still stand or have been re-erected; and though most of the marble facing has long collapsed from the buildings, all among the dunes, along the shore, and in heaps among the honeysuckle bushes and sweet-smelling shrubs, there are piles of broken polished marble, deep honey-yellow, speckled grey, icy white, dark sea-green, and flecked and meaty reddish-purple.

The Severan Forum and Basilica, which are joined, are so big that they are overwhelming; and indeed, to judge from drawings which aim to reconstruct the buildings, the original effect must have been not only grand but grandly vulgar – the copious multi-coloured marble, the lapidary inscriptions with letters over two feet high topping the tall columns, the rows of Nereid and Medusa heads between the arches. But the carved pilasters in the Basilica are strange and beautiful in themselves as they stand – broad-hipped and full-thighed women, Bacchic figures posturing and plundering, spirals of humans, animals, vine scrolls and foliage clusters, all spilling out and fountaining upwards in sensual profusion to the high tops of their Corinthian capitals; and between them two red granite columns soar up to act as bases for a pair of winged griffins on whose backs rests part of the roof of the apse. All are part of a conception both luxurious and supremely self-confident, with an eastern rather than a Latin inspiration.

The harbour, into which the stream of the Wadi Lebda trickles sluggishly or not at all in summer, swollen and red after rain in the winter, is thickly silted up, with a bar at the sea mouth of pure white sand, where I sometimes picked up stray coins. Herons and gulls haunt it, among the stained, twisted, muddy or dusty bushes, and in spring the higher ground all round it is full of wild flowers and blossoming yellow bushes very like gorse. Round it are the ruins of one lighthouse and possibly another, a temple, and on the eastern side long rows of quays and warehouses, below which are the mooring bollards. Big though the harbour was (twenty-four acres), its real importance can't have lasted very long, for the wadi brought down tons of choking mud, and from the other side the sea pushed up its thin barrier of sand. Like so much of Severan Leptis, here was an impressive project which in the end brought more trouble than glory to the city, for the exuberant building programme drained the local treasury dry; and the more obvious the splendours became, the more tempting Leptis grew as a prize to be harried and looted by the native tribes inland, such as the Austuriani, who two centuries later were to turn their attention to the Greek cities of Cyrenaica, when their attacks were recorded by Synesius.

A track from the main road just east of the main entrance leads to the eastern side of the harbour, and beyond it to the newly excavated amphitheatre, far bigger but far more ruinous than that of Annobal Rufus. It was by this track that we camped early in 1966, well beyond the fence which the Department of Antiquities put up in a moment of supererogatory zeal; we quite openly slithered under it, and were never challenged. Here, overlooking the harbour wall and the sea, our only visitors were shepherd boys who desultorily looked after their sheep and goats in the fitful grassland that stretches south to the main road. Sometimes they were a bit of a nuisance, peering into the van as we were having a meal or breathing down our necks as we lay in the sun and tried to read, but always amiably so. All of them ranged between five and ten years old, and they enthusiastically played football and catch with us and with Caroline, who had her seventh birthday at Leptis. One day they even more enthusiastically tore their ragged clothes off and scampered into the sea (it was a warm January day) when Caroline went swimming; and they brought us coins which they had picked up round about, asking ludicrous prices but always settling in the end for reasonable ones. The kind of molesting and stoning which other foreigners were always reciting at length to us was never our experience – but then Ali, Mahmoud, and co. were very young, and our attempts to snub them were as cheerful as their attempts to spy on us. On our last day, Ali, the most persistent of them, came and brought us a bunch of daffodils with which to say goodbye.

Back in the city proper, a wilderness of columns, and of heaped masonry overtopping dunes under which well over half Leptis must still lie, stretches past the Forum Vetus, or Old Forum, the Severan Forum and Basilica, a Christian church and several temples, to the Market and, beyond that, the theatre of Annobal Rufus. The market-place, with its restored circular kiosk (originally one of a pair) and its colonnade of Corinthian columns, looks like some vision of antiquity by Chirico: the golden limestone stands out almost painfully sharply against the deep blue sky, and the shadows can be menacing. Here, on certain days and in certain moods, as elsewhere at Leptis, one can suddenly seem almost stiflingly trapped in some past moment: the effect, perhaps, of the glare from the stone, the heat, the aromatic smells of the vegetation, the buzzing of insects. Even on days when there is a fuming, sand-laden wind blowing in from the desert, the fact that the city lies in its own low coastal plain at sea-level means that it can have its own weather, protected and still.

Some of the stone counters which stand between the columns of the market's portico are deeply scored on their upper surfaces and edges, presumably from years of knife-sharpening; and on one side stands a block with its outer face polished smooth and incised on it the lengths of standard measures. For verisimilitude, this sort of detail perhaps doesn't match what one finds at Pompeii, but at Leptis one is likely to be alone, and the advantages of solitary brooding on such things far outweigh a dozen better-preserved things seen in the company of a press of dutiful fellow-tourists.

From the top of the auditorium of the theatre, behind the market, you can get one of the best general views of Leptis, looking across the tops of columns of a temple dedicated to the deified emperors, and on, across dunes and scrub, to the sea, usually flecked if only a little with white against its sunny indigo or its rain-washed green, for a blustery wind tends to lift from the north in the afternoon even in summer, and this stretch of the Mediterranean is not always as placid as people tend to imagine, But in the morning in July or August it can be almost completely still and oily-smooth, the best time both for swimming and for exploring its pools and crannies among fallen masonry.

Leptis, at the height of its Severan prosperity, must have been as much a city of pleasure as of trade, with its races and animal-baiting in the Hippodrome and Amphitheatre to the east, its plays in the central theatre, its athletic contests in the palaestra next to the Hadrianic Baths, and the Baths themselves. These centre on a large open swimming-bath, round which stand columns of pink breccia marble. By it is a central hall, from which lead entrances to cold baths, a warm room, a hot room, and the sweat baths, all of them faced with marble and ornamented in niches with statues; some of these statues can be seen in the rather unimpressive museum which lies across the main road at Leptis, others are in the Castello Museum in Tripoli. A few have been put back in what are supposed to have been their proper positions. Near the baths are lavatories with keyhole seats cut in the marble.

But large and luxurious though the whole scheme of the Baths was and is, I always found greater interest in the so-called 'Hunting Baths' which lie almost hidden among dunes until one stumbles on them, to the west of Leptis towards Homs and close to the sea. The oddest thing about these is that their roofs are vaulted and domed, and until one grasps that this is an example of experimental architecture in the fourth century it is easy to imagine that these Islamic-looking cupolas are truly Islamic, or even that they're merely modern protective cover for what lies within them. They are a forerunner, indeed, of so much Arabic architecture that one sees elsewhere in Libya, particularly the simple white domes of the *marabouts* or holy-men's tombs. Inside the Hunting Baths are the wall-paintings which give them their name: representations of men spearing leopards, in a context which seems to indicate that this is animal-baiting rather than true hunting (though one poor fellow, his head foreshortened as he crouches on hands and knees, as grotesque and deliquescent as a Francis Bacon figure is being bloodily mauled by a leopard who has broken his spear). Elsewhere there are more peaceful and pastoral scenes; boats rowed along rivers where men fish or go coursing from villas along the banks; ducks, ibises, and dogs.

There was presumably pleasure, too, in brothels, and some sign of these can be seen in the dozen or so phallic carvings which I found in several parts of Leptis: some of them unequivocal penises and scrotums, others elaborately-carved amalgams of phallus-nosed centaurs, phalluses whose hindquarters are bulls, rearing snakes whose significance is obvious, and a sign-language of eyes and crabs less obvious but tempting to speculate about. The best of these can be seen along and near the Via Triunfale, mainly in the direction of the Baths, which may indicate that the Baths were a favourite place for assignations and sexual appetites, as they are in Tokyo today.

South of the main road, among eucalyptuses planted by the Italians or seeded wild from the original trees, is a whole vast area of ruined cisterns and barrages which held and controlled Leptis's water supply. Some of the vaulted cisterns are, in fact, hardly ruined at all, and their great humps, now covered with earth and overgrown with scrub, were enthusiastically used as deliberate hazards by some of the garrison motor-cycle trialists in 1950 until I managed to divert the course: one of my inexplicable duties as an R.A.E.C. instructor was to help organize these trials, and I spent a lot of time on such occasions ferreting about in this Roman water system. It reminded me of long, boring afternoons on the cricket field at school, when I was generally put in some fielding position so remote that I could profitably get on with studying butterflies or grasshoppers.

Leptis was a revelation to me at twenty, of a sun-illuminated, classical, Mediterranean world which I had never even glimpsed before. Ruins, sea, and in myself a feeling of great energy, seemed to combine in a flood which I poured into poems which boiled

with George Barkerisms, thundered with adolescent sexual alle-
gories, and turned my whole experience of Leptis and of Libya
into phantasmagoric shapes. At a cooler level, there seemed to be
a kind of justice in the fact that I was there, for Septimius Severus,
born in the city, had died on the northern frontier of the Roman
Empire, at York: I am a Yorkshireman, and indeed as a child I
had several times had pointed out to me 'Severus's tomb', a big
tumulus which lay not far from my aunt's house in Severus Avenue at Acomb, just outside York. The fact that this tump very
likely has nothing at all to do with the emperor doesn't matter:
the juxtaposition of myself with Severan Leptis Magna seemed
right. Ever since I was seven I have been almost obsessively devoted to the past and the things of the past. On my seventh birthday, my favourite uncle gave me a Roman silver *denarius*, and from
that time on I became an antiquarian magpie. And at Leptis I
secured my most glittering treasure.

Walking along the shore from Homs to Leptis soon after my
arrival in 1950, I noticed the green glint of some corroded metal
among the pebbles in the bottom of a rock-pool formed by the
tumbled masonry below the Forum Vetus. Scooping it out, I saw
it was a small Roman coin of a fourth-century type. I burrowed
about in the pool and emerged, after about half an hour, with
twenty-nine coins. Harry Scammell was keen to join in, when I
told him about my haul, and the next afternoon we went together
and pulled out a hundred or so between us. This was towards the
beginning of July. From then until about mid-September we
spent almost every afternoon at the pool, and a full day whenever
we could manage it. We sat in the pool or perched on the rocks,
stripped down to bathing suits, and our backs and necks turned to
the colour of teak. As we went on, we found that we had to pry
farther and farther into the crannies between the rocks, until our
fingers were puffy and raw; but almost every handful produced –
among silt, small shells, and the occasional furious crab – a few
coins. There were also fragments of gold filigree, a glass bead, a
game-counter, and lead bosses and staples which after a time we
took to be all that remained of the wooden box in which the hoard
had originally been placed.

For it was a hoard indeed. By the middle of September the
waves were growing stronger, and it became impossible to go on

searching: every wave would engulf us, knocking out of our hands, unless we were very careful, whatever we had dredged up from the bottom. But by then we had recovered 7,800 bronze coins. Each evening we would unload the day's finds into a solution of vinegar and water – our amateur substitute for a museum laboratory's electrolytic methods – and start work on cleaning our earlier discoveries. Many of the coins turned out to have become corroded into mere blanks, but many more yielded at least some information. With the help of Seaby's *Catalogue of Roman Coins* we managed to identify a good proportion, and found that the range extended from a single coin of Titus (A.D. 79–81) to several of Theodosius I (A.D. 379–395), with the main group covering the fourth-century emperors.

The problem was, what were we to do with our hoard? It was natural that our first instinct was to hang on to them – but how were we to divide up the spoils? And in any case we both took archaeology seriously enough to realize that the proper place for what we had found was a museum, where there would be proper care and publication. We spent until early 1951 cleaning and identifying the coins, and then decided to approach Caputo, the old Italian curator of the museum in Tripoli. But before this we found that, despite our reticence about the hoard (we didn't want anyone else treasure-seeking on our preserve), the news had somehow leaked out: someone in the public-relations branch of the army got in touch with us, and Harry and I were doggedly posed for a photograph standing behind our loot. The picture was eventually published in the *Sunday Ghibli*, with the news that we had donated the hoard to be a part of the future national museum of independent Libya. Caputo carried away our neatly-labelled bags and trays without much show of emotion – our Italian and his English were inadequate for any lengthy exchanges – and that was the last we saw of the Leptis Hoard.

But that is not the end of the story. Fifteen years later, when I returned to Leptis, with my wife and two of our children, our first goal after settling in was the pool – its whereabouts clearly printed on my memory, dreamt about, daydreamed about. The winter sea didn't make conditions ideal, but it was less fierce than the September one which had frustrated Harry and me. Standing at the top of the low cliff by the Forum Vetus, I was worried at first by the large amount of seaweed which had crowded in among the blocks of masonry, but when we clambered down we found it not too difficult to shift. After a few sterile handfuls of silt, I came up with the first coin; then Caroline with a second, and my wife with a third. Within an hour we had found sixty coins and a bronze finger-ring. The pool was still yielding its treasure; and presumably would go on yielding it to the assiduous searcher. But I am loth to give more precise directions than I've already given, since I feel I have proprietary rights in the place. Another visit, a year later in January 1967, yielded over a hundred more coins.

I would feel less proprietary about it if it hadn't turned out that the original hoard of 7,800 had disappeared without trace. In April 1966 I was in the Castello Museum in Tripoli, where all Tripolitanian antiquities are now centred, and ran into Ali Salaam, the Antiquities Department supervisor from Tocra, who introduced me to a visiting Algerian archaeologist who was working on a hoard of 20,000 coins from Sabratha. I told him about the Leptis hoard, and said that I would like to find out where it was and whether anything had been published on it. The Algerian was much taken with my account, but puzzled that he had never heard of such a hoard. So he got hold of one of the Italian curators, who was equally puzzled. Gradually, it seemed likely that Caputo, getting old and careless, had kept no proper record, and that the stuff had got stowed away in some inaccessible cupboard or chest during the move to the Castello Museum. There was a distinctly furtive and embarrassed air about the whole proceedings; and though the Italian promised to do everything he could to trace the coins, and I believe he meant it, I have never heard another word about them. It may be that they found their way, *via* Caputo, back to Leptis and are lost in the museum there. But as far as I am concerned they have vanished completely, and the only record is that yellowing military publicity photograph and the 160-odd further coins we retrieved from the pool in 1966 and 1967.

I have already hinted that Libya is a country calculated to invite antiquarian serendipity. But at a more serious archaeological level I think I have found only one actually new site, unless I count El Haniya (see Chapter 7) which was already known but the extent and importance of which had been underestimated. This site was near Kassala, my second garrison in Tripolitania, where I was posted after five months in Homs. Across the main Tripoli–Homs road, which runs in front of the barracks, a track leads through lemon-groves and past small pre-Fascist Italian farm-houses to some open scrub and dune country, a good place for Melissa, my Labrador bitch, to run about. Here, a couple of miles or so from Kassala, I began to notice mounds of rubble and scatters of pottery among the dunes. The pottery was of that black-glazed type imitating Greek wares which is fairly common on early Roman sites in Tripolitania and which is easily confused with the 'real' thing. Then coins began to turn up, late Ptolemaic ones, which I had never seen at Leptis: these are things one associates more with Cyrenaica. The whole site was extremely confused, but it seemed to me that these were the remains of a settlement more extensive than a villa, and that there were indications of perhaps a dozen small buildings.

When I had decided that the place was worth reporting, I went to the museum in Tripoli, and found that by chance C. N. Johns, then Controller of Antiquities for Cyrenaica, was visiting Tripoli. With him were a couple of young archaeologists over from England, who had been working on pottery in the museum. I told them my tale, and the following day we drove out to Kassala and then went on foot to the site – the only way. Johns looked at the pottery and coins, walked over the mounds of rubble in that brisk manner that distinguishes the professional archaeologist from the amateur beachcomber, and pronounced the place to be an early Romano–Punic (or Punico–Roman) settlement, unnamed and unindicated on the maps. So far as I know it still lacks a name. But at least it is now a recorded dot, and I have made my small contribution to knowledge.

I did what I could at Kassala to interest the garrison in the past that lay about them, and with rather more success than one might imagine. In the unit library I rigged up an exhibition of pottery, coins, worked flints, maps, diagrams, photographs, with labor-iously ill-typed sheets of information. I even organized a bus-trip to Leptis, which was only sixty-odd miles away but which hardly any of the troops had even seen. These voluntary activities in the end saved me from some tedious military trouble. Just before I was due to leave Kassala for return to England and demob., an officious warrant officer at the Army Education Centre in Tripoli decided that it was time the unit library had a stock-check. I had never checked anything when I took over the library, and when the investigation had finished it turned out that over £20 worth of books was missing. I could feel the demob. gates closing on me, and smelt Courts of Inquiry, reprimands, pay-stops, and the rest.

But apparently at some early stage the library's, and my, deficiencies were reported to the C.O. at Kassala, a remote and to me almost entirely unknown figure. I was summoned before him, and together we went down to the library. There, among the unread novels of Virginia Woolf and the unreadable memoirs of statesmen and colonial governors, my archaeological exhibition was laid out. 'What's all this?' asked the C.O. It turned out – as I already suspected – that he had never been in the library since I joined the unit, and indeed had perhaps never been in it before that. He began to become animated. It seemed that he took an interest in such things, had even wielded a spade in India or somewhere (perhaps, in some spell of respite from boring duties, under the severe military direction of Mortimer Wheeler), and had found no one to share his enthusiasm. I don't know how my activities had escaped him: it goes to show, I suppose, the unfillable gap, even in a small unit, between officers and N.C.O.s. And a twenty-year-old Education sergeant, with all the remoteness that that implies, was not calculated to arouse the curiosity of a hawk-faced military engineer and lieutenant-colonel. Anyway, my footling book-deficiencies were quickly forgotten as he pressed me to tell him about my Romano-Punic site. I left the unit within a couple of weeks, with a testimonial written by the C.O. in my paybook which would have guaranteed me a long life in the service if I had so wished. How he squared the library business with the Army Education Centre I don't know, but I often wonder whether he strode over to my site to do a bit of ferreting about after my departure. Antiquarianism is a great leveller.

Kassala Barracks was nothing but a barracks, fifteen miles from Tripoli and about half a mile from the sea. It housed the 1st Infantry Workshops, R.E.M.E., and in general had little to recommend it. The NAAFI in the late evening would swell with the mournful dirge, sung to the well-known tune:

> This is my story
> This is my song,
> Been in Kassala
> Too bloody long.

There was also a jest current that Kassala's substitute for wine, women and song was rum, bum and mouth-organ. Certainly there was a lot of heavy evening drinking and a certain amount of untender buggery, but this was understandable in a society cut off from towns and women. Tripoli, though not at all far away, could only be visited in the special leave trucks at week-ends, or by cadging a lift from someone on duty. No one took any interest in the Arabs who worked in the camp, most of whom lived in a small hamlet down by the sea among the palm trees. But I struck up a genial relationship with Mukhtar, a small, wrinkled, middle-aged man who swept up the Sergeants' Mess and who sprayed the floors almost ankle-deep in liquid D.D.T. I used to go down to the hamlet and sit outside his hut on a mat while we ate pomegranates and oranges and drank water out of earthenware pitchers. Mukhtar had seen the foreigners move in and out of Kassala Barracks so many times over the years that I think he was sometimes confused: Italians, Germans, British, all merged into one common group of employers. He had a theory that the Italians and the Arabs had large stomachs and the Germans and the British small ones. But he seemed to be making this case for the British solely on the evidence of my small appetite (small, certainly, when faced with a steaming, tongue-lacerating pile of Mukhtar's lovingly prepared *kous-kous*), so I don't imagine he had done much research into the Germans and Italians either.

When I left Kassala, and Tripolitania, in July 1951, I was in a confused state: glad at the thought of getting out of the army and going up to Oxford, miserable at leaving a country which had been a revelation to me. I imagined, without any real conviction, that one day I would return, but practical sense eventually convinced me that this could hardly happen. After all, what would I do for a living there? So that when the University of Libya advertised for an assistant professor of English in early 1965, it seemed a message

✳ 19

destined for me alone. The B.B.C. behaved with surprising sympathy, allowing me two years 'Special Unpaid Leave of Absence', though colleagues and friends were puzzled: to chuck up my attractive and secure job on *The Listener* to go to a country many people had hardly heard of and most people couldn't place on the map seemed an act, to two or three, of almost Rimbaudesque extravagance. 'El Thwaite and his Senussi,' they laughed. But off we went.

2   Euhesperides, Berenike, Benghazi

I CAN hear old Hough's boozy voice booming up from the balcony of the flat below: it's Friday, the Muslim holiday, and so he's off work and getting drunk. All round, the polyglot voices of children swim up through the warm evening air: Greeks, Italians, Egyptians, Palestinians, Iraqis, Indians, Libyans. Living right in the centre of Benghazi, in a tenement built in 1948 but with an air of decay better suited to 1848, we are cut off from the solid enclaves of British and Americans at Fueihat and the outer villas. Old Hough is our only fellow-countryman within shouting distance, and after sixteen-odd years here he's a Benghazi fixture.

There's a breeze from the sea, warm and damp and carrying the characteristic Benghazi smell which I now have to concentrate on to notice: dust, tobacco, spoiled fruit and vegetables, urine, cats, and inevitably one's own sweat. There's something altogether liquescent or deliquescent about Benghazi: a water city. The natural formation of the land and the man-made formation of the old and new harbours have fashioned it into a peninsula, and the third harbour, the inner one, is itself an enclosure of the sea. The *sebkhas* (salt-pans), which fill to their brims with water when it rains in the winter and become lakes, at all times are long sleeves of shallow salt, puddles or ponds where water-birds congregate. Pink flamingoes arrive in December and stand huddled together in the middle. The smell of the *sebkhas* is rank; the sewage and rubbish of the shanties along the Sharia el Mellaha are discharged and thrown into the Sebkha Selmani. But north-east of the city there are true lagoons, fringed with palm trees and dunes. Among them are two fresh-water lakes, known to the English-speaking as the Blue Lagoon and Rommel's Pool; or to call them by their correct names, Ain Zeiana and Bu Dzira.

Summer evenings in the middle of Benghazi are quieter than one might expect in a capital city. Voices shrill up from the street or from 9th August Square, the *muezzin* swell out their competitive, answering cries, and there's a dull rumble of cars and car-horns. Someone somewhere plays a guitar, and I can hear the signature-tunes of Radio Cairo and Radio Libya contending. But it's all, in many ways, like a country town. Tripoli is the metropolis, over 600 miles to the west, across sand which has effectively formed a frontier for centuries between Tripolitania and Cyrenaica. The eastern administrative capital, 130 miles away, is Libya's Canberra or Brasilia: Beida. Benghazi lies uneasily between, run-down, proud, ignored by the King since Ibrahim Shalhi was assassinated here in 1954, a place of decay and impotence. Benghazi has a sentimental regard for its own importance; but whatever importance it really has is in its past.

That past is found most remotely and yet most poignantly on the north-eastern edge of the town, between the Sebkha Selmani and the far side of the cemetery of Sidi Abeid. Here is the site of Euhesperides. One of my favourite solitary occupations was anti-quarian beachcombing here, with nothing to disturb me but the occasional pi-dog. This ancient Greek predecessor of Benghazi lies on both sides of the road: half under the cemetery, half under what is now waste land and an unofficial rubbish-dump for the modern city.

The first Greek settlers here came from Cyrene or Barca some time before 515 B.C. When they founded the city of Euhesperides the Sebkha Selmani was evidently a lagoon deep enough to take small vessels, and it must have communicated directly with what is now the inner harbour of Benghazi; this communication being finally blocked by the Turks in the late nineteenth century when they built the causeway to Berka. But long before that – probably before the third century B.C. – the lagoon had apparently silted up so much that the city was transferred to a site right on the sea-shore, on the promontory separating the sea from the lagoon. This was the city of Berenike, which I shall deal with later.

The remains of Euhesperides above ground are so exiguous that most people in Benghazi, whether Libyan or foreign, are unaware of the place. From the road, one can see the old city mound inside the cemetery, partly cut away by quarrying and partly eroded. Here there are collapsing walls of stone and mud-brick, mud floors, and a litter of Islamic tombs superimposed. On the other side of the road there stretches away, down to the *sebkha*, a confusion of piles of donkey and goat hooves, the carcasses of camels and donkeys, goatskins drying in the sun among the piles of evaporated

✳ 22

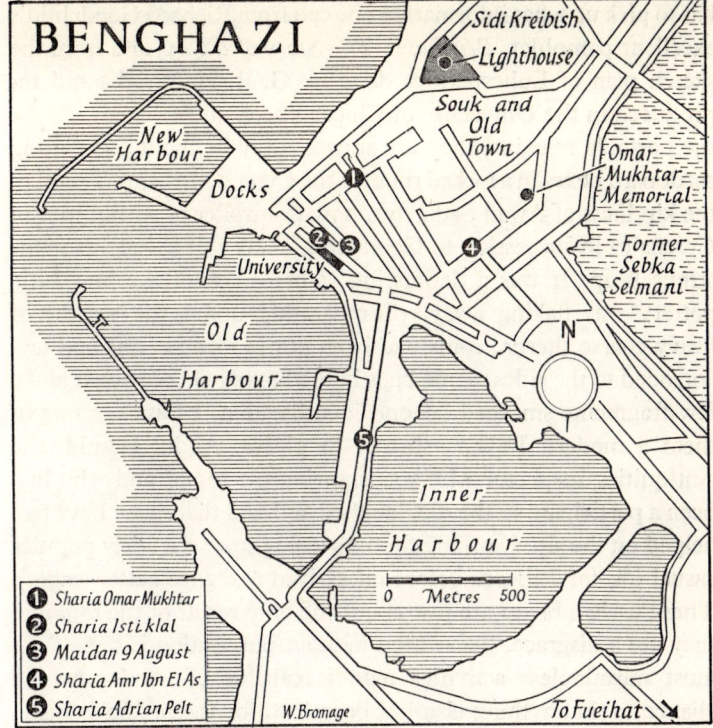

BENGHAZI

Sidi Kreibish
Lighthouse

Souk and
Old
Town

New
Harbour

Docks

Omar
Mukhtar
Memorial

Former
Sebka
Selmani

University

Old

Harbour

N

Inner

Harbour

0   Metres   500

1 Sharia Omar Mukhtar
2 Sharia Istiklal
3 Maidan 9 August
4 Sharia Amr Ibn El As
5 Sharia Adrian Pelt

W. Bromage

To Fueihat

salt used for curing them, rusting heaps of jerry-cans, tips of beer
bottles, and the gutted hulks of abandoned cars. Among all these
one can trace a few foundations of streets and some pavements
of pebble mosaic. On a hot day the smell is pretty appalling,
and my children, after a few bouts of treasure-hunting there,
became reluctant to join me. Lucy, aged four, simply called
Euhesperides (admittedly a mouthful for a four-year-old) 'the
smelly place'.

Smelly place or not, it has a great deal to reveal. When the
R.A.F. was taking aerial photographs of the area – not, originally,
for archaeological purposes but simply by way of routine – the
complete layout of the ancient city became visible, with streets,
building-blocks, and even the city wall. On the basis of this, excavations were carried out within the cemetery of Sidi Abeid in
1952–3 by C. N. Johns of the Department of Antiquities. Unfortunately no excavation report has ever been published, and one

✳ 23

has to pick up what information one can from Richard Goodchild's excellent pamphlet, *Benghazi: The Story of a City*, and from the sketch plan of Euhesperides done by G. R. H. Wright and reproduced in the University of Chicago book on Ptolemais. As for the portable remains, they are stowed away in about 300 rotting cardboard boxes in a locked room at the Cyrene Museum. Through the kindness of Awad Sadawiya, now Controller of Antiquities in Cyrenaica in succession to Goodchild, I was able to see this monstrous heap. It was a depressing sight: much of the fine Attic pottery was flaking away, disintegrating under the weight of heavy coarse sherds; coins had been put in tobacco-tins and had corroded to the sides; some bags in the boxes held only dust and a few fragments smashed beyond identification. I found in one of them a modern Italian ash-tray in pieces: Abdul Hamid, the Antiquities Inspector who was showing me round and who had been a participant in the dig, laughed and said that many boys had helped on the site (working for archaeologists was a fairly popular casual job for Libyans before oil arrived and gave better wages). These useless boxes are just about the only result of the dig, and they are a disgrace. Excavation without publication is one of the most meaningless activities man is capable of. And now the chance to do anything else has been lost, for the *sebkha* is being completely filled in by government contractors, and there is no point in resuming work at Sidi Abeid without knowing properly what has already been done and discovered.

My own beachcombing was equally unsystematic, but I never attempted to dig at all. Everything I found was on the surface. My first forays were over the waste ground between the modern road and the *sebkha*. It was odd to walk between rank piles of rubbish and to find among them sherd after sherd of fourth- and fifth-century B.C. pottery and coins of the same period. This pottery was brilliantly hard glazed black, often with geometrical patterns (meanders and stripes) on the red biscuit. There were fluted handles of jugs and bases of cups, the bases usually bearing palmette stamps. The coins when I picked them up were just light green lumps, encrusted with grit, but stewing in a solution of vinegar and water (the mixture I had used on the Leptis coins), followed by assiduous but gentle picking with the point and blade of a penknife, generally revealed something: the head

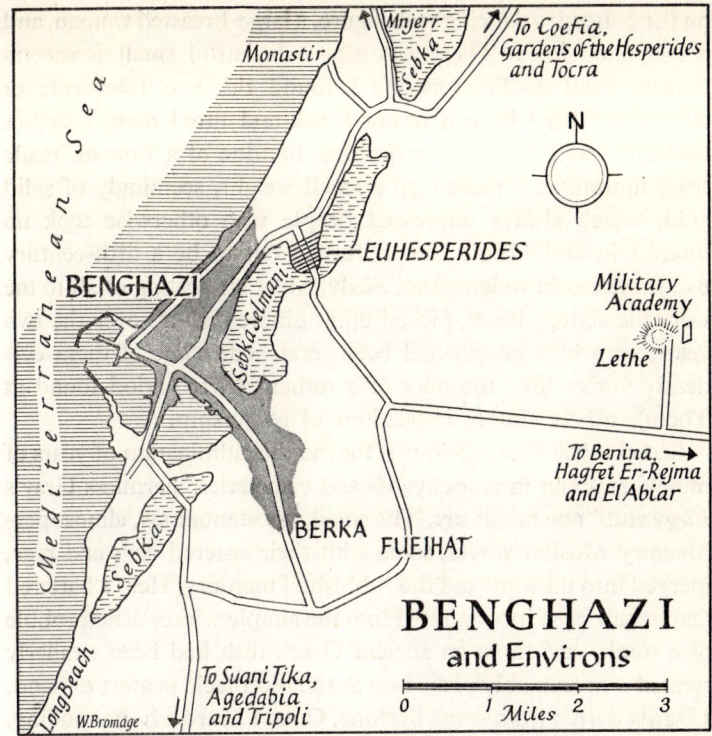

Mnjerr

Monastir

To Coefia,
Gardens of the Hesperides
and Tocra

N

Mediterranean Sea

Sebka

EUHESPERIDES

BENGHAZI

Sebka Selmani

Military
Academy

Lethe

To Benina,
Hagfet Er-Rejma
and El Abiar

BERKA

FUEIHAT

Sebka

BENGHAZI
and Environs

Long Beach

To Suani Tika,
Agedabia
and Tripoli

W.Bromage

0   1 Miles 2   3

of Cyrene, and on the reverse a lyre, a horse, a palm tree, the letters KYPA (for the Cyrene mint-mark), or an eagle.

The Sidi Abeid part of the site was even more rewarding. I had been told that special permission was needed for non-Muslims to enter the cemetery, and that this was bound to be refused, but in fact I never had any difficulty. I used to present myself at the gate, politely ask the *ghaffir*, with my prepared Arabic phrase, whether it was possible to look at the tombs, and walk through unhindered. When I emerged, an hour or so later, my shirt-front bulging with pottery, I always felt guilty; but the *ghaffir* must have thought I was a harmless lunatic, for he never challenged me and was always affable.

At Sidi Abeid there had been much less levelling and consequent disturbance, so the finds were proportionately less damaged. It was here that I found a few more or less whole things (a lamp, a wine-cup, some small bowls), and some figure-painting

✳ 25

on the pottery: a dancing male figure, a large-breasted woman, and a chapleted head. There was also a beautiful small terracotta figurine-head of Persephone: I found the two fragments of what must have been a recent break and fitted them together perfectly. And there was a headless figurine of a woman, made from limestone. I picked up a small weight, seemingly of solid gold, which always impressed people who otherwise took no interest in antiquities: later it turned out to be a fifth-century B.C. bronze coin weight from Sicily. Most interesting of all to me were the sixteen bases, picked up at different times over the two years, on which *graffiti* had been scratched: some of them evidently votive (like the ones of a rather earlier period found at Tocra), others simply indications of ownership.

Searching at Sidi Abeid was for me the culmination of years of moscying about in churchyards and cemeteries: harmless Gray's *Elegy* stuff, one might say. The small, unostentatious, almost perfunctory Muslim graves, some with their tattered flags and rags, merged into the sand and the rubbish of masonry. Here a battered teapot had been incorporated into the simple whitewashed rubble of a tomb, and there an ancient Greek dish had been similarly treated – presumably picked up as the receptacle nearest to hand. Lizards darted from stone to stone. Once I heard a heavy puffing, like an old man chuntering away to himself, and found it was an adder weaving backwards and forwards in front of its hole, short, thick, puffy, and angry at my disturbance. There were often a few pi-dogs at one end of the cemetery, but all I needed to do to drive them away was to bend for a stone, and before my hand had reached the ground they would slink rapidly off. Only once did I ever see any other human visitors and they were workmen carrying blocks of limestone.

There are better-preserved and far more spectacular ruins in Libya – Cyrene, Apollonia, Leptis, Sabratha – but for me Euhesperides is the archetypal ancient site, full of reminders that everything passes, and other sermons in stones. The fact that it has not been built on since it was deserted some time before 200 B.C. is one reason for its uniqueness: elsewhere one wades through a jumble of periods, with Roman pressing on Greek and Byzantine on Roman, with restoration – as at Cyrene in particular – confusing the whole gallimaufry of styles. At Euhesperides there are simply the scavenged, pathetic remnants of a town that lasted for perhaps three hundred years and was then deserted for ever.

Berenike, the successor of Euhesperides, has been almost completely swallowed up by modern Benghazi. It stretched along the seashore from – approximately – the Berenice Cinema to somewhere beyond the prison and the lighthouse, the latter standing in the middle of the cemetery of Sidi Kreibish. Building-construction in this area generally turns something up, but not as much as one might expect. I kept an eye on some foundations being dug just off Sharia Omar Mukhtar, and a couple of large cisterns of the Roman period came to light; but the work had pressed on before anything could be done except for some hasty measuring. As at Euhesperides, the most fruitful area lies under the cemetery, where I watched two mosaic pavements being lifted by the Department of Antiquities for removal to Cyrene. And I found Ptolemaic and Roman coins, lamps and sherds, on the slopes of the great heap of Muslim graves above which the lighthouse stands. It was near here, in a part now under water, that the Beecheys, on their 1821–2 expedition, describe a place:

> Where a bank of 20 or 30 feet (more or less) is formed of the rubbish of one of the ancient cities, coins and gems are continually washed down in rainy weather; and the inhabitants of Benghazi repair in crowds to the beach, after storms, and sift the earth which falls away from the cliff, disposing of whatever they may find to the few Europeans of the place.

These Europeans included the consuls of the time, such as George Dennis and de Bourville.

There seems to have been a settlement at Berenike from about 247 B.C. until the Arab invasion under Amr Ibn el-As in the middle of the seventh century A.D. But the earliest extant building in Benghazi is far later than this, and no one knows how much of the original is left: the mosque of Giama el-Kebir in the Maidan Baladiya, constructed in the early sixteenth century and much altered by both Turks and Italians. Altogether, Benghazi has nothing of historical architectural interest, and little of architectural merit. This isn't to say that its buildings lack charm, but it is a charm glimpsed in details, often hidden away. Down the Souk Ethalam, for example, there are some solid and primitive

✳ 27

arches at the entrances of private houses or leading down cul-de-sac alleys; and along the seafront near Sidi Kreibish there are some decaying, fly-blown houses of the Turkish period which somehow escaped the shelling and bombardment of the war. They have heavy carved wooden doors, which we could find, too, in the narrow streets running behind our flat in Sharia Misurata, along with some good Turkish porch-details.

A few public buildings of the early Italian period (1912–30) managed to survive the war. Most of them try to combine Italian notions with a supposed native quality, and in a curious way these hybrids sometimes work. The former railway station, for example, now the Public Works Department, looks like someone's half-remembered idea of the Alhambra. Perhaps this odd building came from an unconscious realization that Benghazi Railway Station was bound to be a bit of a joke anyway. Rail transport in Cyrenaica never properly got started, and the attempt by the Libyan government after independence to keep it going was an expensive mistake. In the end – until the railway finally closed early in 1966 – the service to Solluch stopped completely and the line to El Merj took one train a week. This wheezing vehicle used to leave at 8.0 a.m. every Friday, and the headmistress of the British School (which adjoined the station in Benghazi) on one occasion received a message from the Chief Stationmaster asking her kindly not to ring the school bell at the usual time of 8.0 a.m. on Fridays but to wait a few minutes until the train had pulled out of the station: the bell had been confusing the engine-driver, who thought that it was the signal to start.

There is another story about Benghazi Railway Station – perhaps *ben trovato* this time. It is said that during the British Military Administration it was decided that the Libyan signal-man at the station ought to be sent on a course to England. The poor man was dispatched, after his undemanding labours in Benghazi, to Clapham Junction, where trains thunder by at the rate of some hundreds a day. Luckily Libyans are not much given to nervous breakdowns.

Other early Italian buildings are the Theatre (now the Berenice Cinema), the University (first the Italian Governor's Palace, and after independence the King's Palace, Al Manar), the Moorish-style Parliament building which is now partly a university text-

✳ 28

book store and which was for a time in the nineteen-thirties the Fascist Headquarters, the lighthouse at Sidi Kreibish, and the huge twin-domed Cathedral. This last was built in 1932, and one was frequently told by British old-stagers that it was popularly known as 'Mae West' – the name giving a pretty clear idea that the old-stagers were old. It is in fact an impressive building externally, and can be seen for miles, both from the sea and the land. The present Bishop of Benghazi, a tiny bright-eyed man without pontifical pomp, stayed in the city throughout the war and did a good deal for not only his fellow-Italian Catholics – or those few who were left after the mass evacuation – but also for the Libyans, most of whom used to get out of the devastated city at night and camp in the plains towards Coefia. For more than two years (September 1940 until November 1942) Benghazi was shelled from the sea, bombed from the air, and changed hands five times: each time the retreating troops, whether Italians, Germans or British, demolished anything that might help the enemy, which meant in effect everything that might keep Benghazi as a bearable place for its inhabitants.

Benghazi since the war has been in a constant state of rebuilding and of consequent turmoil, accelerated particularly since the large-scale plans which followed on the big government revenues from oil beginning in the late nineteen-fifties. Big offices and blocks of flats line the main streets of Istiklal and Omar Mukhtar, and they stretch out all along the dual carriageway to Berka. Pipes for water, sewage and cables are laid and relaid, so that the pavements – when they exist – and the roads are always piled high with earth and debris. Water and open sewers gush out. Streets bewilderingly become one-way for a week, two-way the next week, and closed the third. New flats, banks, offices, hotels, are rushed up with rickety scaffolding and breeze-blocks, with a handmade slap-dashness fascinating to watch but not much good for living in. The air is thick with builders' dust and heavy with hammerings and bangings. Yet the impression, oddly, is one of a town running downhill, itself turning into a Euhesperides.

But having already used the word 'charm' of the place, I must justify myself. It is partly the charm of an overgrown village, the sense one has of neighbourliness, of being on at least nodding terms with hundreds of familiar faces. I could never walk out of the flat without in a few minutes coming across students, friends and acquaintances: I must have spent dozens of Benghazi hours in pavement greetings, chats and farewells. Then there is the physical charm common to most coastal Mediterranean towns, with the sea glimpsed in more than one direction, ships anchored in the harbour, and the strong breeze from the sea coming almost unhindered, it seems, from Greece. And there is the effect of strong clear sunlight on the colour-washed walls of pink, yellow, white and green, the surfaces themselves often crumbling and flaking but the whole composition united in its squares and angles like a cubist painting. The view from the roof of our block was such a composition, framed to the north by the sea and to the south-east by the distant line of the Jebel behind Benina. It is a tourists' platitude that foreign squalor is more attractive than British industrial and suburban grimness, but Benghazi, though in some sense decaying and certainly untidy, is not a squalid town.

Real poverty exists on the edge of the town, in the shanties made from corrugated iron and packing-cases at El Kish and close to the road beyond Sidi Abeid, and in other huts tucked away near the ring-road, where they contrast sharply with the well-stocked Fuiehat villas mainly inhabited by foreigners: British and American oil-company people, generally, with a sprinkling of rich Libyans. These villas have proliferated in the past half-dozen years. On the whole they are unimpressive one-storey flat-roofed buildings outside, and the constant change of tenancy means that the gardens are not often well kept up, though we had English friends who managed through hard labour and lots of watering to make their place blossom with bougainvillea and mimosa. The rents are high and are still climbing: some are still let unfurnished for £70 a month, but on the whole they have climbed to £90, £100, £120. Many of the landlords are Benghazi shop-keepers who shrewdly bought up plots of land cheaply at the beginning of the oil boom, rushed up one villa with borrowed money, let it at a high rent, and with the proceeds went on to build more. They are now extremely rich men, but most of them still live modestly in or near their shops in the *Souk*, preferring the high walls and inward-turned privacy of their little courtyard houses to the open spaces of Fuiehat.

The shops of Benghazi are equally profitable, though they

ignore window displays and such salesmanship. Almost everything can be bought, at a price: all imported goods carry a heavy Libyan duty, and shopkeepers are capricious about the figures they add to this, so it's as well to shop around. The best place for fresh fruit and vegetables, and largely unfrequented by foreigners, is the Fondouk. This is the arcaded and colonnaded building on the road out towards Sabri, Sidi Abeid and Tocra, where the hired microbuses and taxis start for Beida, Tripoli and Cairo. In the square round which the arcades run, the wholesale merchants put out their baskets of spinach, tomatoes, cucumbers, aubergines, courgettes, melons, apples, lemons and so on. All these, together with big bags of potatoes and onions, can be bought in bulk, but if you want smaller quantities you can always find someone willing to sell. The stuff is fresh and in good condition if you get there early enough – 8.30 or so in the morning – and you pay a reasonable price, much lower than the retail greengrocers in the central vegetable market off Sharia Omar Mukhtar, and low enough in comparison with the smaller Benghazi shops to be worth the weekly visit. Tinned goods and 'long life' heat-treated milk can also be bought here in bulk and are economical.

Outside the courtyard, in the colonnade and beyond it, there are rush-mat and basket-sellers, hardware stalls, and an open-air pottery market. The pottery market is well worth seeing: great heaps of crocks lying in the sand. Unfortunately there are no pottery-kilns left in Cyrenaica, but big plain amphorae and smaller earthenware jugs, all unglazed, are sent over from Tarhuna and Kussabat in Tripolitania, and dark-brown and apple-green glazed dishes from Tunisia. Most of these are attractive and some of them are useful, though plastic and metal containers – for example the ubiquitous jerry-can – are driving out the traditional earthenware as water vessels. Pottery is one thing in Benghazi which it is acceptable to haggle over – haggling being oddly alien to the place, a fact which many foreigners in this Middle Eastern context find difficult to believe. I bought a tall stately amphora and a big Tunisian dish for 50 piastres (ten shillings), but the original price asked was a pound.

The *Souk* itself, which starts at the Maidan Baladiya and stretches down to the Fondouk, may be a disappointment to the traveller who knows the *Souks* of, say, Tripoli or Tunis. The traditional craftsmen are of a limited range – limited, in fact, to leather-workers and base metalworkers – and so the carpets, clothes and jewellery one sees all come from elsewhere: Tripoli, Misurata, Cairo, Tunis, Jordan. Some of the knick-knacks which are meant to appeal to foreigners even come from Singapore, India and Japan. But the Souk Ethalam (the covered *souk*), despite the foreignness of many of its goods, has an atmosphere of its own, particularly at mid-morning or just after nightfall. (Avoid Fridays, however, when everything is closed and the place is simply a shuttered and roofed alleyway.) In particular there are the itinerant sellers of gold, striding up and down from shop to shop, their arms festooned with bangles, bracelets, many-stranded necklaces, rings, pendants, and large gold fish. All these are dowry-components, usually bought piece by piece over the years until a worthy accumulation has been made. The men who offer them shout and badger and jingle their wares, but I never actually saw a sale being made.

The shoes and sandals, locally made, are good: Bedouin boots, stout but soft, in yellow leather and often tooled in red, are the prototype of the British army (and, later, fashionable) desert boots; and the simple one-thonged sandals are cheap and stand up to a lot of wear even in rough country.

But altogether Benghazi is happily not geared to the souvenir-hunter. Artificial-silk cushion covers and wall-hangings with *A Souvenir of Libya* worked in coloured embroidery are perhaps the thin end of the wedge, but I noticed that most of these seemed to go to Libyans: I don't know why, unless this was another manifestation of the patriotism that makes miniature Libyan flags such a popular fixture in Libyan cars. The most expensive – but this time attractive – local products are equally popular among foreigners and among those Libyans who can afford them: I mean the carpets and rugs made at the Government Rug Factory in Benghazi. This lies off the road between Berka and El Kish, and has as its present adviser an Egyptian textile-designer, who is married to an English painter. Their house, filled with their own creations, is one of the most attractive in Benghazi. The carpets and rugs made by the factory are based on traditional Islamic motifs and also earlier ones, such as the Byzantine mosaic from Gast Lebia. All use natural dyes – browns, black and white.

✳ 32

Among the foreign communities of Benghazi, the British have been the biggest, simply because of the army units stationed there. When all British troops were withdrawn from Tripolitania, what was left was the R.A.F. station at El Adhem, just south of Tobruk, and the Benghazi-based men: in my time these consisted of a battalion of Dragoon Guards (armoured cars now, but with a certain amount of money and sentiment still expended on horses), a detachment of the Royal Anglian Regiment, together with various support units – R.E., R.E.M.E., R.A.O.C., and so on. The two barracks are Wavell and D'Aosta, large bleak encampments on the perimeter of the town. There was also a Forces Broadcasting Station at Wavell, a kindergarten and school at D'Aosta, the British Military Hospital, and a NAAFI club ('The Ace of Clubs') in Benghazi itself: sometimes I used to walk by this at night, look through the windows, and feel oddly nostalgic at seeing all those large, pink, raw-faced men standing about drinking Whitbreads and Double Diamonds. But not for long.

The army community in Benghazi as I saw it seemed just as isolated from the country, just as caught up in its own concerns, as the ones I had known from the inside in Tripolitania. Soldiers and their families were catered for in such a way that they could be completely self-sufficient, and it was said that there was one army wife who had lived at Wavell for two years without ever having gone out of the camp gates. The Forces Broadcasting Station, along with its staple of pop-music from 7.0 a.m. – 9.0 a.m. and from 5.0 p.m.–11.0 p.m. ('*Sincerely Yours*, Ted King's own *personal* selection from the new releases', etc.), carried announcements of local military activities: tombola, a Beatnik Evening at the Junior Ranks Club, a dance at the Officers' Mess, D'Aosta, a whist-drive at the Ace of Clubs, a snowball tombola. This odd enclave of Benghazi society has now vanished, since the British garrison was withdrawn after the Middle East war, the last remnants leaving at the beginning of 1968.

The largest remaining part of the British community are the oil people, mainly B.P. They, of course, are much more radically concerned with Libya, in so far as they have helped to make it the rich country it is, and also because many of the men spend a lot of their time deep in the desert, away from even the mild fleshpots of Benghazi. The oil companies rent and furnish their villas, put

✳ 33

air-conditioning in, provide them with a club at Fueihat with swimming-pool, tennis courts, squash courts and a bar, run a bus to and from the British School for their children (the British School being a part-foundation of B.P.'s), maintain their own clinic with their own doctor. The men are intelligent, their wives a friendly and agreeable lot, though they seem to spend a great deal of time involved in such null activities as the International Women's Club, playing bridge and having Coffee Mornings ('CHILDREN ARE DELIGHTFUL . . . AT HOME' reads the invitation). Our children found us miserably lacking in the amenities provided by B.P. children to whose parties they went – home movies and such elaborations.

Then there are the engineers and construction people. Some are involved in the reconstruction of the harbour, some (like old Hough) are long-term employees of the Libyan government, dating back to the early years of independence or even before. Others are brought in on a shorter-term contract basis, for example to do the electrical wiring in the new Central Post Office: our predecessor in the flat was such a man, a cheerful cockney in his mid-twenties who was earning £3,500 a year and enjoying a life which would have been unthinkable in the static, pay-freeze atmosphere of Britain. There are radiocommunications engineers who form a lifeline with the oilmen in the desert, and others who staff Control at Benina Airport.

Finally comes a miscellany of accountants (to Kingdom of Libya Airlines, for example), bank officials (Barclays D.C.O. and the Bank of North Africa), Embassy officials and secretaries, British Council officers, and teachers: but the last are naturally subsumed in the next chapter. I can speak most closely of the British Embassy and the British Council, apart from the teachers. The Embassy (represented by a Consul-General) is in the usual anomalous governmental position found in Libya, in that it has to play second-fiddle to the Embassy in Tripoli – where the Ambassador is based – and yet has the closest lines of communication with the new administrative capital in Beida: the Consul-General usually has to visit Beida once a week, staying while he does so at the Cyrene cottage which I describe elsewhere. The purely Benghazi activities are of smaller importance. From the point of view of the British residents, the high point of the year is predictably the Queen's official birthday in June, when the Embassy lawn – one of the few lawns in Benghazi – is thronged with a motley collection of one's fellow-countrymen: in June 1966, for example, I spent most of my time talking to the Director of Antiquities for Cyrenaica and the King's Bee-Keeper. The British Embassy Residence is one of the more attractive of the early Italian buildings of Benghazi; it was originally the Italian military commander's house.

After the British minority, the Greeks, Egyptians, Levantines, and Italians follow. The Greeks are mainly Alexandrians and Cairenes in origin, and most of them have never even visited Greece. They are very successful merchants, shopkeepers, insurance and shipping agents, and hotel-keepers, and they are multi-lingual: to a poor linguist like myself, it was an impressive experience to watch the manager of the Modern Grocery Store, a lugubriously-moustached Alexandrian Greek, dealing in quick succession with customers in English, Arabic, Italian, French and Greek. There is an Orthodox Church and one priest. Most of our neighbours in the block were Greeks. They lived a full-throated public life on their balconies, carrying on long declamatory conversations from floor to floor, dealing with their children in alternate bursts of lavish affection and frenzied physical pummelling. Sometimes in the evening they built fires on their balconies and cooked *souvlakia*, and they played the same throbbing, soul-scouring Greek records over and over again on the gramophone.

The Egyptians draw on the widest range of jobs, being everything from skilled workmen to university professors. Like most non-Libyan Arabs – if indeed one can call them Arabs – they show, whether openly or in confidence, contempt for Libya and Libyans, whom they consider to be a backward, stupid, lazy lot. They are not, by and large, popular, despite the barrage of Nasserite propaganda on Radio Cairo and in the window displays of the Arab Cultural Centre, and despite the assiduous work by Egyptian teachers in the schools. Wherever one went in Cyrenaica, schoolchildren would parrot Egyptian propaganda; I remember a boy at Tocra demonstrating with his arms the size and power of Nasser's world, and how nothing could stand in his way. Yet the older Libyans distrust the man, despite the subtle tugs of sympathy felt through the whole notion of 'Pan-Arabism' and the

✳ 35

feelings of unity aroused by the Palestine Liberation Army and the Israel problem generally, all of which centred on Egyptian inspiration and energy. In the university, the Egyptians were involved in internecine warfare to an extent which made our own quarrels in the English Department seem both trivial and gentlemanly. The Professor of History and the Professor of Arabic spoke with great bitterness and heat about one another at Faculty Council meetings: the Professor of Philosophy was not on speaking terms at all with the Professor of Sociology. At the end of one academic year two Egyptian heads of department and one assistant professor were summarily sacked by the Libyan authorities, without explanation: for intriguing, for intelligence work, for making derogatory references to the Libyan monarchy – no one really seemed to know but everyone had his own story. Altogether Egyptians are in a more delicate position than other foreigners; sharing so much, and for that very reason being ill-judged by those with whom they share. One might, I suppose, draw some sort of parallel with attitudes to Americans in Britain.

The Italians form a much smaller part of the foreign population in Benghazi than they do in Tripoli. Their Cyrenaican reputation has never recovered from the brutalities of colonization and the Senussi Wars, and yet it is the Italian inheritance that is superficially most obvious: the architecture, the engineering of the roads, the farms, even the language that comes most naturally to almost any middle-aged or older Cyrenaican when talking to a foreigner. My Italian is clumsy and haphazard, but it is a great deal better than my Arabic, and there were several times when to use Italian was the only way to communicate. But it is true to say that present-day Italian influence on Cyrenaica in general and Benghazi in particular is minimal. They have their cathedral, their schools, a few tourists – a larger number than from other European countries – and not much beyond that.

Finally there are the French, concentrated on the air-crews of Kingdom of Libya Airlines; the Germans, engineers working for Mannesmann, the construction company, or for Volkswagen workshops; the Poles, mainly outside Benghazi and building the new town of El Merj; and a handful of almost everything else, from Dutch to Algerian and from Nigerian to Cypriot. There is a growing body of Indian and Pakistani doctors, and Nationalist Chinese

✳ 36

Sergeants Harry Scammell
and Anthony Thwaite with
the Leptis coin-hoard, 1950

Leptis Magna, the theatre

Benghazi, the Fondouk

Taken from our roof in
Benghazi

General view of Jaghbub

Graffiti at Tocra

doctors and nurses. An Indian family lived in the flat immediately facing ours across Sharia Misurata, and even more than the Greeks they lived their lives at full pitch. For several months I went to Arabic evening-classes with a group of Indian and Pakistani doctors, and matters sometimes turned nasty: one Indian protested loudly and passionately to our Libyan teacher – 'Sir, I implore you, go more slowly. You are unaware that our Pakistani colleagues are here at an unfair advantage, in that they are already thoroughly familiar with the Arabic syllabary. You should not cater for them alone but regard' – a wide sweep of his arm, taking in myself and the Indians – 'those of us who are not so equipped.' It was this sort of border dispute that helped to make me gradually give up Arabic lessons. Still, the sub-continental *saris* of the doctors' wives brightened up the streets of Benghazi, and their open femininity was a healthy corrective to the shrouded Libyan womanhood.

All this comment on foreign minorities might give the idea that Benghazi is a cosmopolitan place, but this would be a misleading impression. The atmosphere is strongly Arab, strongly Cyrenai-can, once one turns aside from Sharia Istiklal and the top end of Sharia Omar Mukhtar. There are those who say that all town life is alien to Cyrenaica, that what is native is Bedouin, nomadic, avoiding the coastal stretches, and in a sense this is true; but on the other hand there have been Arab towns on the Mediterranean since at least the fifteenth and sixteenth centuries A.D., and wherever these original settlers came from – Turkey, Misurata in Tripolitania, even, at a later date, Cretan Muslims such as settled at Apollonia – what has emerged is a homogeneous Cyrenaican society, with alien Arabs and alien Westerners on the periphery. If you walk down Sharia Amr Ibn el-As towards Omar Mukhtar's memorial, or beyond it towards the Fondouk, and take any of the small turnings to the left, you find yourself in a place and an atmosphere that has hardly changed since della Cella and the Beechey brothers visited Benghazi in the early nineteenth century. I say 'walk' advisedly, because these narrow streets were not intended for cars. Early on, I got my van stuck several times when vainly looking for addresses in these parts; without warning, an alley suddenly takes a sharp-angled turn into a cul-de-sac, and the car is surrounded by small boys beating a gleeful tattoo on the windows and jumping on the bumpers as you hotly try to do a three-point-turn between blank walls and crumbling Turkish buttresses.

It was on one such afternoon, after I had peevishly extricated myself and was driving back to the main road, that I came upon a sight unusual enough to have aroused the interest of not only myself but the whole street. A small and very embarrassed-looking policeman in his white summer uniform was shepherding along a tall flamboyantly-dressed Negress, her bright brocaded shawls thrown back from her face: she was pouting and flouncing her contempt for the whole business, while behind the two of them a crowd of eighty or so children leaped about, jeering and catcalling. A prostitute was being taken into custody. The street of the prostitutes was close by, opposite the north end of the Fondouk, but it isn't a subject one hears much about. For simply mentioning that the street existed, Gwyn Williams's *Green Mountain* – the book of an enthusiast, thoroughly pro-Cyrenaican and sometimes almost fulsome in its loving delineation of the country – was banned in the eastern province (though I was amused to see it on the shelves of the British Council Library in Tripoli, underlining again the sense one has of two countries in uneasy alliance). To ban prostitution and to maintain that it does not exist does not stop it from existing. I heard stories of university students sometimes 'buying' a woman in common for a few months, installing her in their lodgings not only for the usual thing but also to do the cooking and washing – a sort of House Mother. But this sounds more like the fly boys in the Commerce Faculty than the dutiful fellows in Arts.

So much – one might say – for night life in Benghazi. But this would not strictly be true. There are indeed cabarets or night clubs, some of them (the Berenice, the Lux) attached to hotels, others (the Riviera, the Olympia) independent. They attract a handful of bored foreigners, usually bachelors up from the desert, but their staple clientèle is Libyan, and so the atmosphere is even more furtive and dingier than their equivalents elsewhere. Drinking expensive whisky while watching a strenuous but mechanical belly-dancer is about as sinful an experience as you will find in Benghazi, and infinitely depressing it is. The civil law in Cyrenaica follows the Islamic law rigidly in its complete ban on the sale and consumption of liquor to and by Libyans, so that any Libyan in these cabarets (unless he is unlikely enough to be drinking Pepsi-Cola) is liable to be prosecuted. In fact the whole place is plunged in such darkness that one cannot see one's neighbour without straining, and the police must consider this brings the proceedings within the bounds of propriety, for I never heard of a police raid on any of them. The cabaret artists – Greeks or Turks on a Mediterranean tour between Cairo and Tunis – tend to stay at the National Hotel, a bleak and comfortless place at the harbour end of Istiklal where I spent my first three weeks in Benghazi. These girls, with their bizarrely dyed hair, teetering high heels, and bottom-hugging skirts, were usually taken up by rich young Libyans in sports cars: among these was the so-called 'Black Prince', a renegade and most un-Senussi-like relation of the King's, who drove a red M.G. and lived in an enormous sentry-patrolled palace outside Benghazi on the Tripoli road – though he must have found Benghazi far too provincial, for the palace was shuttered and apparently deserted for most of the year.

Because of the drink laws, drinking by the minority of Libyans who touch the stuff tends to be not only furtive but brutish and violent. The beaches closest to the town – beyond Giuliana on the west and round Monastir and Mnjerr on the east – are favourite places for cars to draw up in the evenings, in the safety of darkness, and for groups of men to start work on a crate of beer or a few bottles of whisky: the sands are littered with bottles, almost always smashed in a final destructive frenzy, and it's as well to avoid these places at night, for fear of getting involved in some boozy brawl. One can almost make it a rule that no Cyrenaican drinks – except to excess. After all, once you have started on the forbidden stuff you might as well go on, and inhibitions and frustrations are released in an orgy of bottle-smashing and quarrel-picking. Down Sharia Misurata was a 'grocer's', to which I give inverted commas because its main stock was liquor and any other stock seemed simply a front. Out of it I watched guilty-looking men emerge with grey-paper parcels, which they would load into cars and go belting off out of town. The shop was run by an Italian, as were the other two drink shops in Benghazi. They sold enough, openly, to foreigners for the *convenances* to be observed, so again the police seemed to keep clear of them. But these drink shops, whether run by Jews or not, were among the prime targets for rioters on June 5th, 1967.

The beaches of Benghazi are among the real amenities of the place, far better than the crowded, club-owned beaches of Tripoli. Many foreigners belong to, and use, the Sailing Club, which has premises and a small beach near the centre, almost opposite the Berenice Hotel; but this is expensive and the beach is unpleasantly full, so we avoided it. Unless one is really devoted to sailing – and such members are in a minority – it is a place to avoid. The best beaches are out of town but not far away by car: 'Long Beach', beyond Giuliana and the municipal and army beaches, is the handiest, but it lacks character. Monastir, reached to the east by a turning just beyond the police-post, is better, with rock-pools, sponges on the shore in winter, and a jetty; but the jetty is sometimes nauseatingly used by lorries dumping sewage, and one may strike a day when this is happening. A little farther on, reached by a sand-road used by the lorries loading sand for filling in the Sebkha Selmani, is Mnjerr, which at times looks almost like the French Riviera: well-tanned elegant bodies, bright beach umbrellas, expensive skin-diving equipment. The French, in fact, mainly Kingdom of Libya Airlines pilots and their wives, give the place this sort of tone, but one doesn't need to compete. There is a steep narrow promontory on the east which gives the name (Mnjerr means 'beak'), and on top of it a small white Islamic tomb nestling among the confused ruins of a fortress, probably Byzantine: the first time I visited Mnjerr I found a large bronze Byzantine coin sitting next to the tomb as if awaiting my arrival. The promontory shelters the beach from the prevailing wind, and one can enjoy good swimming and sun-bathing.

But the best swimming places need a little more searching out. By the *zawia* (mosque and Koranic school) just before Driana there is a marvellous beach, with some evidence of a Byzantine settlement for those who are bored by just lying about; and the fact that this is almost twenty miles from Benghazi should not be off-putting, because twenty miles on the coast-road in Cyrenaica quickly seems to be no more than five miles in England. Distances no longer seem to matter, and anyway the roads are so free of traffic. If one wants fresh-water swimming, there is a fine place

✳ 40

much nearer than Driana and not far beyond the Mnjerr turning: a large bush on the right by the last petrol-station out of Benghazi before El Merj is the landmark to aim for. The skimpiest of tracks – sometimes disappearing completely among flat weathered rock, quite safe to drive on – leads after half a mile or so to a broad spring-fed lake, surrounded by cliffs, and fringed with reeds. The water is brackish but not at all unpleasant to swim in. There may be one or two local boys swimming, but no one else – certainly no foreigners.

'Blue Lagoon' – Ain Zeiana – is better-known but never crowded, though I became almost neurotic in my avoidance of places where even one other car had drawn up: it was at Ain Zeiana that I am reported to have burst out one afternoon with 'The place is like *Brighton*' when we arrived to find two other families within sight. At any rate, it lives up to the name the British gave it when they first arrived during the war: the blue is astonishingly intense, and the dazzling white sand and elegant palm trees combine to make it a northerner's vision of the Mediterranean. Someone has conveniently jammed the trunk of a palm tree between the rocks at the edge at one point, and this makes a good diving board.

Our favourite swimming place of all was on the opposite side of Benghazi, reached by turning off the Tripoli road to the right just before coming to Tika: this was Suani Tika, approached along a smooth sand track with only one or two soft and potentially dangerous patches, the track sometimes running straight across salt-flats where I could feel like a racing-driver. It was uncanny to see, across these flats, whole villages, groves of trees and wide lakes looming up and shimmering on the horizon; on our first visit it took us some time to realize that these were mirages, they were so clear and matter-of-fact. The point to aim for is a small concrete tower, which at first seems itself to be a mirage, but gradually resolves itself into a solid and unromantic ruin – the tower of a temporary wartime aerodrome, now disappeared. Below this the white sands stretch clear and clean for as far as the eye can see. In many visits, we saw other people only twice – once a Libyan family almost out of sight, and once a couple of youths in a small boat with an outboard motor. They were fishing Libyan-fashion; that is to say, dumping bits of explosive in the sea and picking up the stunned fish. I have never been enough of a sports-man to feel very strongly about this, though purists always seem extravagantly shocked, as if killing fish by blowing them up was somehow less humane, as well as less skilful, than getting a hook embedded in their jaws. At any rate, these youths were friendly and gave us a bucketful of fish: mullet, very delicious.

There may come a time, I suppose, when Benghazi will really become 'developed' as a tourist centre, and all these beaches will be bought up by *Clubs Méditerranées* and the like: the local news-papers and the Department of Tourism handouts seem to be pressing that way. But they have been pressing that way for so many years that I've come to think – and to hope – that it is all windy talk. Benghazi's hotels are few and unsatisfactory. Only the Benghazi Palace Hotel, seemingly suspended above the water on the far side of the inner harbour, can offer something of what tourists want; and it is extremely expensive.

Hired transport is difficult to come by, and public transport is confined to Benghazi itself. Without accommodation and trans-port, tourism on a large scale can hardly begin. Tripolitania is ripe for exploitation, though even there there are enormous problems; but Cyrenaica, luckily for those who do manage to get there, seems likely to remain unspoiled for as far into the future as one can guess. I hope time does not disprove me.

3   Difficulture

'LIBYANIZATION' – the process of handing over to Libyans jobs previously done by foreigners – is not a word that has gained much currency in the country. But the fact is true enough, and all that is stopping it from being completed is time and training. When the British Military Administration took over in 1943, they found a people starved of almost all education by the Turks and the Italians. Even routine clerking jobs had been largely denied to the Libyans: it was rare to find a Libyan mechanic, impossible to find a Libyan engineer, except one or two (such as the future Prime Minister, Mustafa Bin Halim) who had been brought up and trained in Egypt and who on the whole remained there until independence. There were no teachers beyond primary-school standard, no doctors, no lawyers (again, except for a handful in Egypt), and the few men who had managed to get into the lower echelons of the Italian administration, such as another future Prime Minister, Mahmud Muntasir, trained in Italy, had been given parochial jobs of little significance.

Some attempt was made by the British, and with some success, to get education on its feet. But it was not really until independence that the groundwork was done to establish schools throughout the populated parts of the country, and not until the oil revenues started to pour in during the 1960s that new school building was properly organized. Now Libya is – in the words of the *Sunday Ghibli* – 'the land of a thousand schools' (978, actually, when I last saw the figures). In the most remote and unlikely parts of the country you suddenly come upon a brand-new school, with its brand-new teacher's one-storey house next door. It may be that these two buildings will form the nucleus of a new village settlement, but at present there is often no other sign of habitation within sight. The children come in from the tents on donkey-back or on foot.

The University of Libya was founded in 1955, to begin with solely in Benghazi, though later a Faculty of Science was opened in Tripoli and there are plans for a Faculty of Medicine there. At

✳ 43

first there was no accommodation problem: after the assassination of his adviser, Ibrahim Shalhi, in Benghazi in October 1954, King Idris was so disgusted with the city that he decided never to live there again, and so the Manar Palace was presented by him to house the new university. The Manar Palace had also been Graziani's residence when governor of Cyrenaica, and it was from the balcony overlooking what is now 9th August Square (named after the date when the Libyan army was formed in 1940) that he used to address his Eritrean troops, the Fascist Youth, and the Blackshirts, in the way described by the Danish traveller, Knud Holmboe, in his book *Desert Encounter*: 'You are Romans fighting against barbarians. Be kind to them, but always be their superiors. Remember that you are Romans.' It was on this same balcony in my time that one of the British lecturers in the Faculty of Commerce, a fellow full of japes, used sometimes to appear and put on a dumb-show Mussolini-parody act. How he was never caught I don't know. Perhaps Libyans, with memories of the past, never glanced up at that balcony.

It was the Faculty of Commerce, in fact, that used the Palace proper, while the Faculty of Arts, for which I worked, was housed in an extension which had been built round three sides of the patio. The acoustics of the lecture-rooms were terrible: a colleague who had worked in several Arab countries said that this was common to them all – tiled floors, a lot of glass, and walls and ceilings bare – and his theory was that half the difficulties among Arabs learning English came from the fact that they never heard more than an approximation of the sounds.

But these rather unsatisfactory buildings are in the process of being replaced. On the western edge of Benghazi, at Gariunis, a new university campus is planned, which is said by its architect – an Englishman, James Cubitt, who has specialized in building universities in emergent countries – to be the biggest single architectural project in the world. It will stretch between the Tripoli road and the sea, taking in administrative and teaching blocks, a huge and radically designed library, dormitory accommodation, a sports ground and swimming-pool, and eventually staff accommodation as well. The plans and model are certainly most impressive, but difficulties lie along the way. One of the earliest problems was that of persuading the herdsmen with grazing

✳ 44

rights there to sell, and the whole business of finding out and dealing with the owners was fraught. Then there was the problem of the amount of wartime explosive which lay about the site under a shallow covering of sand.

Labour is not easy to find either, and here, as elsewhere in Libya, foreign construction workers will have to be brought in: at Driana I came across Lebanese at work on houses for the Idris Housing Scheme, a grandiose building plan aimed at providing both for the homeless of Benghazi and Tripoli and for settling the Bedouin of the hinterland. There were many Egyptian building workers in Benghazi, and others at Jaghbub: Sudanese in some places, Poles at Beida, Bulgarians making the new sports arena on the edge of Berka; Yugoslavs, Greeks and Italians making roads. Tenders for the new university were advertised in London, Paris, Rome, and Bonn. And who – the question was more often implicit than spoken – will be the students? The potential in a country with less than one and a half million inhabitants isn't limitless.

The Arts students were not on the whole a very bright lot, academically. Getting some sort of higher education doesn't, in Libya, mean vaulting the terrible entrance-examination hurdles it means in Japan, for example. One sometimes felt that the government was eager to press into academic life anyone who could put pen to paper, in its efforts to staff and 'Libyanize' the country. But in any case the Arts Faculty had its own difficulties, because we were a long way down in the cream/milk stakes. What happens is this. At the end of his secondary-school course (and this can be at any age, because a lot of men go to evening classes at the secondary schools at the end of a day's work), a candidate takes his *Taujihia* or leaving-certificate. On the results of this, a compulsory and state-directed filtering process begins. The top percentage, a tiny number, are sent to study abroad, generally in Germany, Britain, Italy, Belgium, or Egypt: many of these are encouraged to read medicine. Next comes the Faculty of Science in Tripoli. Then a certain number of appropriate men are siphoned off to train as army officers at the Military Academy, from which they emerge looking so poised, smart, and arrogant that it never surprises me that *coups* in the Middle East are usually organized by young officers. After that the Faculties of Commerce

✳ 45

and of Law get their rake-off. And finally – just above the teachers' training colleges – the Faculty of Arts and Education receives its dip.

The only exceptions in all this are the women. They are not sent abroad (except – and this very rarely – *after* a university course in Libya); few of them go to the Faculty of Science because science-teaching in the girls' secondary schools is inadequate; none, of course, go to the Military Academy, and traditionally Commerce and Law are not geared to receive them. So we did tend to get the brightest women in the country, and they leavened the lump. One year, I remember, the annual prizes in the English Department, based on the results of the end-of-year examinations went in three out of four cases to women. As in Japan, the men used to belittle this sort of achievement with such remarks as, 'Well, they have much more time to study than we do: they just sit about at home' (to which I used to reply, 'Rather than sit about in cafés, you mean?'), or 'They have less to think about'.

Among all the Muslim countries, Libya is one of the least emancipated in its attitude towards women. Our girl students were bright, but they also had to be tough to have got where they had, fighting against all the traditional pressures which would have kept them at home to follow the severely restricted routine of an ordinary Libyan woman. While we were in Libya we read Hannah Gavron's sociological study, *The Captive Wife*, and the assumptions and attitudes – as well as the title itself – seemed to have a bizarre irony. How could English women regard themselves as in any way *captive* when compared with Libyan women? In the towns, it is still the rule rather than the exception for women of all classes, rich and professional, poor and uneducated, to be veiled on the rare occasions when they appear in public, either with the voluminous *barracan* (white in Tripoli, multi-coloured in Benghazi) or, among the few who wear Western clothes, with a black net completely enveloping the face. The *barracan* is held against the face so that a fold, kept in place with one hand, veils only one eye. When both hands are occupied – with using a broom, for example – the fold is held by the teeth, and this is how we used to see the women at work sweeping the floor of the Central Post Office.

That a woman's place is in the home is interpreted strictly: she

✳ 46

does not do the shopping or take her children to hospital, unless her husband or her husband's brother or some other male relative isn't available; she never goes to a café or a cinema, and very rarely on a social visit, unless to other members of the family and only then when accompanied by her husband. Marriages are, of course, always arranged, and the wedding ceremony is a dual affair: a series of entirely separate male and female gatherings, with all the ratification organized by the senior males, and the social celebrations strictly segregated. Home itself is made into what to Western eyes would seem a prison. One of the university administrators took matters to the lengths of painting the windows of his flat, so that not only could no one look in but his wife could not look out.

The wife of the University Rector was a daughter of the Prime Minister, and had broken away from the system to the extent that she taught at the girls' secondary school in Benghazi; yet even she – a woman who was in many ways sophisticated, and with a far more highly trained mind than most Libyan men, let alone women – was not a keen supporter of emancipation. She told us that she thought Libyan women were not yet ready for freedom, and that any advance in that direction should be extremely gradual. The government has paid lip-service to female emancipation, so that ostensibly women have the vote; but the proportion actually using it is tiny. There was, in 1965, a Women's Emancipation Day, which was commemorated with a special postage stamp, the design of which was unfortunate: a rather loathsome-looking grub emerging from a chrysalis.

Some foreign women in Benghazi are continually complaining of the unwelcome attentions they get in the streets or on the beaches. Sometimes I felt that they secretly got some sort of *frisson* out of the ogling, the whispers, and the unmannerly suggestions, but it is true that a certain amount of exhibitionism went on – though Ann was subjected less to this sort of thing than in fact she has been in England. It shouldn't be surprising that men who are used to the public exclusion of women find the sight of bare-faced, bare-armed, bare-legged foreigners provocative. Given this sort of society, there seems to be less overt homosexuality than we found in Japan, with its 'gay' bars and all-girl shows (of which girls are the greatest devotees). Libyan girls at the university tended to go about in their own buzzing little groups; no doubt they felt stronger and more able to cope when banded together.

Many of the girl-students used to arrive each morning at the University veiled. As soon as they got inside the gates, they would pull off these hideous black nets, which always remind me of bee-keepers' hoods, and act normally, though on the whole with a reserve and lack of vivacity which is not native to them but which is 'appropriate' behaviour when there are men about. They tend to dress in an unbecomingly lumpish way, but this used to be the charge against female undergraduates in Britain too until quite recently. Dress shops in Benghazi are few, because the local population of women doesn't dress in a Western way, and the foreign women would rather buy new clothes when they are on leave in their own countries.

Arabic–English is a special variety of its own. In *The World of Dew*, D. J. Enright drew attention to the differences he noticed between the un-Englishisms he found in Japan and in Egypt: 'My experience has been that those of the Egyptians are predominantly comic in spirit – slovenly, a bit brutish, cavalier, unpredictable but yielding to elucidation, orotund and occasionally superb. Those of the Japanese, on the other hand, are predominantly tragic – contorted, agonized, tight-lipped, sometimes baffling, consistent and insistent, and occasionally poetic in a gently sad sort of way.' One thing the two languages share is a sound-confusion: in the case of the Japanese, L and R ('Lever Brothels Limited'), among the Arabs P and B. So round the corner from our flat in Benghazi a BLUMPER had hung out his sign, and I remember the examination candidate who referred to that famous London landmark, Pig Pen. One student, stubbornly insisting on the indistinguishability of the two sounds, went so far as to challenge me to distinguish between 'bray' and 'pray' without some such context as 'The donkey brays and the clergyman prays'.

But the confusions of Libyan students can sometimes be felicitous and even poetic. 'Libya is a country of agriculture and difficulture', for example – how aptly that sums up the country's problems. And the confusion of the nuances of a single, simple word can be seen very attractively in this comment written by a fourth-year student: 'Most of Mr Forster's novels are rather short but *A Passage to India* is rather tall.'

There is not much 'creative' writing among the students, even in their own language: Libya is not a land of poets (though the main hall of the Arts Faculty is named after Rafiq, a modern Libyan poet who spent most of his life abroad), and publication in Cairo or Beirut – since Libya has no publishing houses which handle fiction or verse – seems impossibly remote. However, the university held one poetry evening where staff and students recited fervently, and the Shakespeare Society (organized by the English Department as a sort of extra-curricular literary group, largely unconnected with Shakespeare) ran a literary competition. All the entries were, of course, in English, and among the non-prizewinners I particularly delighted in Awad Wanis's 'A Short Visit to England', which celebrated his recent stay in Croydon:

I lived with a family which was very nice
Mr & Mrs McDonnel who gave to me advice.
There, in Croydon, is holy pleasure in your eye,
By its green pastures, almost its own sky!
The beauty of Croydon, silent and bare,
Bright and glittering in the smokeless air.

A recent reading of Wordworth's sonnet 'On Westminster Bridge' may account for something there, but so far as I know Wanis had never read Blake. Much more astonishing, and not at all funny, was an entry by a second-year student who had generally been taken by the staff – and by the students too – to be a bit of an idiot. Big, shambling, grinning, incoherent, given to large demonstrative gestures in class, he bent sweatily over the microphone in the hall and read, slowly and deliberately:

There is nothing to see in the sky.
Except four aeroplanes.
Smoke, fires, kites fly.
Clouds and white grains.

It is a sudden fearful attack.
The enemy conquered at noon.
The army has turned back.
Vehicles will arrive soon.

✳ 49

Wars require destruction.
Peace is better and harmony.
But there is interaction.
What we call temporary.

Vice and virtue are adversaries.
What will be defeated?
I fear there are no dispensaries.
In which they are treated.

Our unanimous award of the first prize to this poem was an unpopular move. The favourite had been a man who was generally
acknowledged by the other students to be the departmental poet:
a tall, handsome, taciturn but smooth character in dark glasses,
who wrote chunks of high-toned and purple stuff with such titles
as 'I and the Sea' and 'My Platonic Love'. Mabrouk, the prize-
winner, was seen by the students to have been chosen for 'political' staff reasons – because he could do with encouragement to
battle with his lunacies, for example, or as a general fillip to the
second year at the expense of their seniors in the fourth year, such
as the dark-glassed poet. No amount of strenuous denial squashed
this. Afterwards I asked Mabrouk whether he had written any
other poems. He hadn't. Having seen his success, would he now
go on writing? He grinned with his enormously wide and mobile
mouth, and replied, 'If there may be a competition next year,
maybe I write one.' He was given, so far as I remember, a large
and hideous photograph-album worked in multi-coloured silk.
Later, he failed his end-of-year examinations. I shall never know
how he managed to construct those strange, oddly punctuated, and
rather poignant quatrains: they were indubitably his own, but
where did they come from?

I have said that Libya is not a land of poets, but I must qualify
that. Libyan 'literature' as such is practically non-existent, but
there is a large amount of folk-poetry and folk-song, and this is
something everyone shares. I went with my daughter Emily on
an Arts Faculty three-day trip to the Jebel, and both in the bus
there and back and under canvas the songs and the ballads hardly
stopped. The Dean had the most capacious memory for these
things: love songs, satirical songs, verse-flytings, nonsense poems
– all of them poured out of him, and he was a good performer. But
everyone could contribute, and some of the best sessions were

when the Dean took on all comers in some cumulative piece of extempore group verse-making, the rhymes and the puns becoming more and more audacious as the poem got longer and longer. Both Arabic prose and Arabic verse tend to be constructed on a basis of 'and', 'and', 'and then', which is a good binder for this sort of serpentine composition, but it does mean that students find it very hard to grasp the principles of punctuation in English; their sentences go on and on, eschewing relative pronouns and commas, sometimes ending with a full stop, sometimes not. Oddly enough, in Libya I began to find myself writing poems using very long sentences. No connection, probably.

The Dean was always reminding people, with a waggish sort of pride, that the Faculty boasted three poets. Apart from myself, there was an Egyptian who was said to have some sort of reputation in the Arab world and who also fancied himself as a scholar: he had been known to introduce himself as 'Professor Sadiq of London University'. He took himself immensely seriously, and obviously regarded the English staff as a lot of amateurish, lightweight undergraduates. The third poet, our upstairs neighbour in the block of flats during our last year, was an Iraqi who looked off-puttingly like Groucho Marx. His one European language was Spanish, which made communication difficult, and as for his verse I was constantly being told (by Egyptian colleagues) that it was fifth-rate. However, I remember a performance he gave at one of the Arts Faculty receptions which seemed to go down well: a long, elaborately chiming-and-rhyming eulogy of the staff, which was greeted at the ends of several stanzas with applause for especially outrageous technical trickery.

These university receptions were crushingly boring. The occasions used to start with us all sitting on the balcony of the Palace in two long lines facing one another, with in between us tables covered with Pepsi-Cola, orangeade, and mineral water. Even a medium sherry would have done everyone a lot of good, but of course this was Cyrenaica, officially the most strictly teetotal of all Muslim states. After about forty-five minutes or an hour of this, we would be ushered by the Dean into the hall, where there were tables laden with stuffed courgettes, stuffed green peppers, chicken, mutton, fish, a concoction of rice, almonds and sultanas, and salads of cucumber and tomato. The Egyptians in particular always ate heartily and grossly, disregarding knives and forks: there is an Arabic saying, 'Good appetite begins at the fingertips'. After fruit and sweetmeats of bran and honey, we were directed back to the balcony where we had glasses of tea and were regaled with speeches. The only man apart from the Dean who ever said anything funny, or even human, on these occasions was the Egyptian Professor of Philosophy, who was reputed by the Libyans to be an agent for Nasser. Whatever the truth of this, he was a lively and cosmopolitan man who refused to subscribe to the droning, incantatory classical Arabic address thought appropriate by all the other professors in these circumstances, and instead spoke briefly and wittily, in colloquial terms. He was popular with the students and disliked by many of his own colleagues. He was married to a very pleasant Scotswoman who had published a book about her marriage to him and their life in Egypt. Altogether, Osman did not fit in with the severer notions of the university, and he did not return in my second year.

The Dean was probably the most remarkable man in the Faculty. Like all the senior administrative officials, and unlike most of the teaching staff, he was a Libyan: youngish, trained at the University of Chicago as a sociologist, quick-minded, energetic, and with no puffed-up self-importance or assumed dignity. He knew precisely what he wanted to get from foreigners, whether Egyptians or Englishmen, though one piece of perhaps symbolic eclecticism struck me: on top of the bookshelf in his office were two objects – a model of the Statue of Liberty and a bust of Lenin.

The English Department suffered from several disabilities, some of them common to most overseas teaching by Englishmen: for example, the rapid turnover of staff and hence a lack of continuity. Most people stayed for only two years (the minimum period guaranteed by the British Council, though in fact two of my colleagues lasted only a year). The first Professor of English was Gwyn Williams, whose book on the Jebel Akhdar, *Green Mountain*, I have already mentioned. Williams was and is a Welsh scholar, a fine translator of Welsh verse, and under him an attempt was made to run the department as a British-style Lang. & Lit. affair, with emphasis on literature. Doomed to failure, of course, and Williams's successor, Bernard Blackstone, who combines literary studies with a selling line in language textbooks, brought much more 'practical' language work in. By the time I arrived, in the interregnum between Blackstone and his successor, we had a staple of language and a top-dressing of literature, sometimes of a bizarre and entirely unsuitable nature. I ploughed through H. G. Wells's *The Invisible Man*, an inheritance from the syllabus I could well have done without, since Wells's extravagantly nudging style and characters who mostly speak broad Sussex formed impenetrable barriers, even supposing the book is worth intensive study at all.

Equally impenetrable, though for different reasons, was *Look Back in Anger*, which some predecessor must have thought would give a lively picture of contemporary British youth. The behaviour and attitudes of Osborne's theatrical characters were beyond the comprehension of young men and women whose notions of rebellion – if they indeed had any, and this was rare – were of a quite different political sort. And what do you do when Jimmy Porter launches into an attack on women making up?

When you see a woman in front of her bedroom mirror, you realize what a refined sort of a butcher she is. Did you ever see some dirty old Arab, sticking his fingers into some mess of lamb fat and gristle? Well, she's just like that . . .

There was much doing of substitution-tables and pattern-practice, much talk of language laboratories. In the process, some of the students did manage to acquire passable English, but it was a struggle and it was not all their fault when they didn't manage. The trouble with Libya, educationally, is that it has no horizons: there is a stifling provincialism about the place – not stifling to me, to whom provincialism was a refreshing escape from metropolitanism, but deadly to people who ought to be omnivorously grabbing, selecting and rejecting everything they can lay their hands on. But what can they lay their hands on? A student in Benghazi finds no theatre, no museum, no art-gallery, no concert-hall or opera-house; the bookshops are few, and those there are would suffer by comparison with a railway bookstall in Heckmondwike; the cinemas hardly ever show a film, from any source, which is of any value. So the whole of his education has to revolve round the university and the university library, with the British Council and the municipal libraries on the periphery if he makes the effort. Cultural starvation means that the mind withers to an organ capable of assimilating and parroting a few necessary facts: thinking and enjoying are functions unconnected with education.

All this has nothing directly to do with the state of English in the university but concerns the whole condition of Libyan education. 'Language', of however intensive and ambitious a sort, isn't going to help much here. I remember a don coming on a tour from England. He was invited by the university to lecture to the students of the English Department, and so for several days we all sat through 'The Nature of Linguistics and its Place in University Studies', 'Phonetics and Phonology', 'Socio-Linguistics: Considerations on the Place of English in the World Today', and 'Descriptive Linguistics in the Grammatical and Lexical Analysis of English'. Unfortunately his matter and manner were completely opaque as far as the students were concerned. After an hour of *'inter alia'*, *'prima facie'*, and so forth, together with a number of oblique attacks on unnamed academics who failed to achieve the proper rigour of linguistic discipline, even the fourth-year students had to admit that *nothing* at all had been understood or taken in – except the minimal amount of Arabic which the professor had used, far too sparingly, by way of illustration; for this eminent linguist was an Arabist as well. The whole episode blighted the morale of the department for some time. If this was 'language', how was anyone ever going to learn anything?

But lack of grasp of the language need not or should not accompany the lack of general knowledge or the inadequate responses that one found. What is the use of even touching on poetry when a third-year specialist is still capable of a judgement phrased in such a way as: 'poetry without rhyme is not good poetry and its effect on readers is very weak and not nice'. Here the ordinary Arabic *mush qwayyis*, 'not nice', is being forced into a mould which can't contain it. Checking with teachers (Egyptians, Iraqis) in other departments which naturally used Arabic as the medium of instruction, I found my impression confirmed: the Libyan student simply hadn't read or thought enough to cope with anything approaching a university course.

Sacking all the Egyptian teachers in the secondary schools and

※ 54

bringing in Englishmen would certainly not alter this, though it would free students from some of the supposed 'rules' they have to absorb at present. For example, one Egyptian has published in Libya a piece of guidance which tells us how to differentiate between verbs in any given social situation: hence one 'begs' or 'prays' a superior, 'tells' an equal, and 'orders' or 'commands' an inferior. Odd stuff from a citizen of a socialist republic, but perhaps Libyans, being more hierarchically minded, lap it up.

Few students had much notion of socialism or any other -ism, anyway. There was a student union, but it lacked any sort of power and had little function. Some students had tried to re-organize it, but this was looked on with suspicion by the authorities; indeed, one of my third-year students – a serious, diligent young man, with nothing of the firebrand about him – had almost been prevented from going to England on the usual month's study-course in the summer, because the Rector thought he was a security risk. He was one of the student union representatives, and had helped to draft a new constitution for the union. The constitution had rather naïvely been constructed on the pattern of such things in Egyptian universities, and unfortunately phrases like 'The aim of the union is to further the revolutionary cause' had been copied verbatim from the original.

This business of the student union has been a sore one for several years, and particularly since January 1964, when several students (who were demonstrating for Libya's full participation in the Cairo Conference) were killed by the Cyrenaican Defence Force (Cydef) in Benghazi. The victims became martyrs and formed a rallying point for all militant student activity in Libya. What the more vigorous voices began to press for was an all-Libya student union, embracing university (including the Islamic one at Beida) and secondary school. This was something neither the university authorities nor the government in general were willing to grant, for such a union would inevitably become the most articulate and powerful political force in a country where political parties are not allowed to exist.

The end of 1966 and the beginning of 1967 saw an upsurge of student activism. At first the disapproval of the students seemed to be directed against a new system of terminal tests which the university senate had introduced. In November, when the first test was introduced, only a handful turned up to take it, but there was no active demonstration. Then at the end of January, with the second test, the trouble began. The real struggle seemed to begin on the week-end of January 28th/29th, when about 300 students sat down in Sharia Istiklal outside the university, blocking the road and stringing black-lettered banners across it: EXPELLD [*sic*] STUDENTS SHOULD BE BACK and HUNGER STRIKE TILL DEATH. This was the consequence of the expulsion of three students, all of them active in the illegal union and one of whom had insulted the Dean of Arts by calling his wife a whore. The police diverted the traffic and swarmed thickly all over the area, keeping pedestrians and cars away so that everyone had to make wide detours. They carried truncheons, revolvers and rifles rather more obviously than usual, but since these weapons are normal issue to Cydef people there was nothing particularly sinister about this.

Over the next few days the numbers thinned out considerably, particularly at night. It was one of the coldest and wettest winters for some years, and sitting in the street, chilled and hungry, needed some will-power. The crisis came when the strikers picketed and tried to prevent other students from going into the university. Apparently one of the Commerce Faculty students, whose father was a commissioner of police, lodged a complaint, and the Cydef acted on this; some people thought it a put-up job, since it made a good excuse for what followed. The police swooped in and carted off a number of the students: reports differed about the numbers, some saying twenty-four, some thirty-eight, some fifty. Others spoke of teachers from the boys' secondary school and 'merchants in the *souk*' being roped in, accused of aiding the students with money 'from a foreign power': Egypt, of course. Most people seemed to think they were put in Benghazi prison, but I was told on good authority that they were confined out at Benina (where the Cydef keeps an airborne striking-force), so that there would be no chance of sympathetic demonstrations outside the prison in town.

There were rumours, too, about when the trial would be held, or whether there would be a trial at all. On February 15th a mob of secondary-school boys tried to march down Istiklal towards Sharia Omar Mukhtar (where the law courts are), were diverted

✳ 56

by the police on to the seafront, and then had a stone-throwing session, reminiscent, it was said, of the January 1964 troubles. The police were all round the secondary school the next day, with their truncheons out and their hoses at the ready. But nothing happened.

Rumours drifted through from Tripoli, Beida, and other centres, and all were of strikes, demonstrations, and scuffles with the police. It was said that a student in Tripoli had been killed, and that the Science Faculty had been closed down there. It was also said that some members of the Majlis had approached the student leaders before the Cydef's punitive action and had offered to make representations to the Prime Minister if the students would go back to work. Yet throughout the whole period there was no mention in the Libyan press or over Radio Libya of what was going on: people listened to the B.B.C. Arabic Service, which carried some news of the troubles, and to Radio Cairo, which naturally gave much publicity to the supposed sufferings of the students under their archaic tyrants.

The strikes and demonstrations had one odd growth, in that Libyan students in London, Bonn and Amsterdam showed their solidarity by demonstrating at the same time. In London they sat down outside the Libyan Embassy in Prince's Gate, and were taken to Bow Street where they were each fined ten shillings: the (British) National Union of Students paid these fines, and the fact was duly reported in *The Times*. Although copies were censored before they reached the Benghazi newsagent, the censor – typically – had torn out the wrong page in some, so the item had a fair amount of circulation. What *The Times* report did not say was that the London students went on sitting for several days after their brothers in Benghazi had given up and gone home (or been arrested): no one, apparently, had got round to sending a cable advising capitulation. And to sit out on a February night in London is a considerably harsher discipline than a similar exercise in Benghazi.

All these activities left the university tense, shaken, and depressed. Numbers gradually picked up at classes, and by the first week in March attendance was more or less normal, though the arrested students had not returned. But throughout it all what was most characteristic was the flurry of rumours, and the sense, too, that nothing was being done to settle the problem. Though it was as well for the members of the English staff to keep quiet – since we were politically as vulnerable as the Egyptians, however scrupulously we behaved – I couldn't help now and then asking questions that might have been construed as dangerous. But I got no closer to the truth, always supposing there was a truth to get close to. One student told me that the whole affair was engineered by the Egyptians, and that for that reason he was keeping well out of it: another (a Tripolitanian) said that it was all the work of 'Cyrenaican secret political organizations', and that therefore no Tripolitanian would touch it – which was palpably false, since one of the ringleaders (how easily one falls into the vocabulary of Authority) was a Tripolitanian law student

Such quasi-political student activity seems muffled and parochial, perhaps, set against similar activity all over the world during the past few years – California, India, France, Japan, China, L.S.E. But for me it seemed quite different from anything I had come across in Japan: different too, from the early 'Ban the Bomb' thrashing-about in which I myself had taken part at Oxford in the mid-nineteen-fifties. Here in Libya it was clearly the frustrated rumblings of an élite which had been denied any political outlet. Yet it is too easy to say 'clearly': nothing from the beginning was clear, precisely because there was no open forum and no public acknowledgement of what was happening or what was at stake. The Libyan Government will have to learn sooner or later that trouble is not avoided by keeping silent. As it was, during the student troubles rumours were far more pernicious than any straight news item could have been. And the events of June 5th, 1967, when the students showed how powerful they could be in mob action, and how uncontrollable, were never reported in the Libyan press or radio. It was left to the English-language *Sunday Ghibli* – normally a lightweight and even frivolous organ – to give, surprisingly, the full facts of that day's rioting; and for this one moment of truth, the paper was suppressed.

4　Hesperidean Places

ALTHOUGH life in Benghazi was relaxed, and we generally found ourselves occupied enough with teaching, reading, writing, shopping, and looking after four children, we felt
cheated if we didn't manage to get out of the place at least once a
week. Close at hand there were the swimming places I have
mentioned, but not much farther there are more evocative sites to
aim for. For an afternoon, we might choose the Gardens of Hesperides, Lethe, or Hagfet er-Rejma: for a whole day, Tocra and
some subsidiary things off the Tocra road, Tolmeita, Asqefar,
or Gasr Jeballa. For the areas deeper into the Jebel Akhdar we
liked to have a couple of days or more, and these come into other
chapters.

After $7\frac{1}{2}$ miles, on the road to Tocra and the Jebel north-east
out of Benghazi, you reach the small village of Coefia. On the left
is a former Italian fort, where in the late nineteen-twenties the
Danish traveller Knud Holmboe saw Cyrenaican prisoners being
hanged in batches. It is now a boys' reformatory, with tall dry-stone
dovecotes built by the boys – like fantastic follies by Gaudi, and
I'd have thought big enough for every pigeon in the eastern province. On the right are a couple of shacks selling soft drinks,
tinned goods, and tomato paste. Just beyond them a minor road
starts out quite well but peters out after a few hundred yards in
the centre of Coefia – chiefly distinguished for its Italian pill-box,
built like a toadstool. Here the road becomes a mere track over
holes and weathered rock, but a hundred yards or so of this
brings one into position to see a group of palm trees on the left
which seem to have most of their trunks below the surface of the
ground. Until you stop the car and walk towards these trees, you
have no idea of the hollow out of which they are growing. This is
the place to aim at.

It's a shock, in the middle of this barren table of sun-baked sand
and flat rocks, suddenly to come upon this lush hollow: a massive
fault in the limestone, fed by springs so that the bottom is thick
with rushes and grasses, on which cattle graze. Round the edge

✳ 59

are fig trees with their ghostly silvery-white bark, wild olives, prickly pears, and some excellent date-palms. On the far side, away from Coefia village, is a cranny in the rocks through which a slimmish person – and even some stouter ones, whom we managed to urge on during repetitions of this favourite trip – can slip and slide down to water level. In the small caves or rock holes on the way, where the springs feed the pool, big black catfish swim in the half-darkness, sometimes caught by a brilliant shaft of sunlight at the right time of day.

The whole area is full of such fertile depressions, but this one – which the local people call El Tara, 'the wonder' – is the most spectacular. And it and its associates are the putative Gardens of Hesperides. The Beechey brothers, on their 1821–2 expedition, were among the first to connect this place with the ancient legend: they write of the depressions being:

several hundred feet in extent, inclosed within steep, and for the most part perpendicular, sides of solid rock, rising sometimes to a height of sixty or seventy feet, or more . . .
It was impossible to walk round the edge of these precipices, looking everywhere for some part less abrupt than the rest, by which we might descend into the gardens beneath, without calling to mind the description given by Scylax of the far-famed garden of the Hesperides.

Both Pliny and Scylax wrote of the garden or gardens, but Pliny (in his *Natural History*, Book V, Chapter 5) is, of course, a later source. Scylax, writing in the fourth century B.C., placed it near the Gulf of Phycus, between Ptolemais and Cyrene; Richard Goodchild takes Phycus to be the modern Zaviet el Hamama, whereas El Haniya seems to me a more likely spot. But in any case there are no such 'gardens' in this coastal area below the Jebel, such as are described by Scylax:

a place eighteen fathoms deep, sunk in the ground and without access, its length and breadth are not less than two stades.
Dense intertwined trees shade it, and include the lotus, apples of every kind, pomegranates, pears, blackberries, vines, myrtles, laurels and ivy.

Although eighteen fathoms (about a hundred feet) is much deeper than the Coefia gardens, two stades (about 350 yards) is a fair guess at their length; and when we later find Pliny writing that 'not far inland from Berenike is the river Lathon, and the sacred wood where the Garden is remembered', we seem to have found the nexus of the two stories.

I shall come to the Lathon, or Lethe, connection in a moment. The Gardens of Hesperides themselves were under the authority of the Hesperides, the four nymphs Aegle, Arethusa, Erytheia, and Hestia. They were appointed to guard the golden apples given by Ge – the earth mother – to Hera on the occasion of her marriage to Zeus. These guardians were blessed with sweet voices, and they were helped in their wardenship by a dragon, Ladon. One of the labours of Hercules was to secure the golden apples, which he did after slaying Ladon or, say others, with the help of Atlas, whom he therefore relieved of the burden of the heavens.

The precise localization of such stories is a late development, and probably the Greek founders of the city they named Euhesperides were simply drawing attention to the similarity between the real 'gardens' they discovered on their doorstep and the imagined ones they thought of as being somewhere remotely to the west. Whatever the explanation, I never felt any doubt that there was something strange, even uncanny, about 'the wonder'. Visit after visit – and it was always one of the showplaces to which we introduced people new to Benghazi – didn't stale the curious atmosphere. It was as if the whole of this green and almost rankly burgeoning hollow had become isolated, frozen, in some trick of time – a golden age. Sometimes the feeling was almost oppressive, and I was reminded of the way in which Miss Moberley and Miss Jourdain described their hallucinatory experiences at Versailles in *An Adventure*.

Even one's modern encounters (not, in Moberley/Jourdain fashion, with ancient Greeks) heightened rather than diminished the effect. Once, in November, I watched a man gathering dates there. He was strapped to the tree with a rope belt, and plucked the ripe fruit with a sickle, dropping it into a bag tied round his waist. He called me over and threw some dates down for me, asking me as he did so whether I was army or civilian. When I told him, he replied with great warmth: '*Qwayyis*. Army no bloody good – too much bullshit. Guard, polish, left right left right. No bloody good.' It turned out that he had fought with Wavell as a volunteer in the Senussi detachment. Certainly he had picked up

✳ 61

a rich store of British military expressions. The dragon and the nymphs had departed, but a disenchanted veteran up a palm tree seemed a proper replacement.

Lethe is more problematical. In some ways the dark hidden springs down the cranny where the catfish swim seem right. There is a strong legendary connection between the Gardens of Hesperides and Lethe – perhaps some such juxtaposition of opposites as Donne's

> We thinke that *Paradise* and *Calvarie*,
> *Christs* Crosse, and *Adams* tree, stood in one place.

Lucan, describing the Lethe in the Benghazi area, wrote (in Nicholas Rowe's eighteenth-century translation):

> Here Lethe's streams, from secret springs below,
> Rise to the light, here heavily, and slow,
> The silent dull forgetful waters flow.

The Coefia waters palpably 'flow'; but even heavier and slower are the waters at the site nowadays called Jokh el-Kebir, a few miles across country from Coefia towards the Benina road. Here – along a turning to the left, just opposite the ruined Italian railway station of 'Lete' – you reach the Military Academy of the Libyan army. The entrance is sporadically guarded, but I never had any difficulty in getting permission to drive through, and I never asked in advance. Just through the entrance, down some steps to the left, you reach the entrance to a cavern, with locked iron gates at the top of the second flight of steps and at the mouth of the cavern itself. A *ghaffir* is always somewhere about, and he will willingly unlock the gates. Before you reach them there is, on a slope just to the left of the steps, an artfully ruined modern stele, inscribed with some sonorous lines from a d'Annunzio poem.

It was here that the Italians in the late nineteen-thirties constructed a Lido, of which no trace remains, except the frail duckboards they built out into the underground lake and the wiring system which feebly lights the waters. The huge craggy entrance to the cavern is impressive, certainly – fig trees splaying out from crannies in the rock above your head, and a feeling of clammy warmth as you descend, suitably dizzying on the approach to oblivion. But, once inside the cavern, first bent low through a rock tunnel, then stepping out across the duckboards, I was disappointed: the water is not only so sluggish as to be stagnant but very shallow too, and the murk under the low-powered electric bulbs is sordid rather than mysterious. The transparent crayfish that crawl listlessly through the few inches of water near the duckboards seem to move in a state of appropriate forgetfulness, but they cannot compensate for the ghostlier presences one expects but doesn't find in this rather depressing hole.

To come out of the cavern and find officer-cadets shinning up and over assault-courses, or trotting up and down in vests and baggy blue shorts, is also lowering. The chief interest at Lethe, really, was for our children, and this consisted of turning the minor nooks and hollows on the way down the steps into the haunts of witches or wild animals or, alternatively, schools. Just beyond the slopes leading to the cavern are some shallow depressions in the sand, spring-fed and still cultivated by men growing spinach and carrots: it is these unimpressive hollows, fertile but lacking all mystery, that Richard Goodchild takes to be the Gardens of Hesperides, but I find this difficult to believe. Just to confuse the matter more, Playfair (in his *Travels in the Footsteps of Bruce*, published in 1877) says:

About ten miles to the eastward [of Benghazi] is the Lake Tritonis, with a small island, where was the Temple of Venus, now Monastir, and to the northward of this, the lake Zeian [Zeiana] or the Beautiful, formerly called that of the Hesperides, into which a stream rising in a small hill above it runs into the sea, which has a communication likewise with the lake, and is the Leithon of Strabo.

But Lake Tritonis, if it can be sited at all, must surely be the ancestor of the present Sebkha Selmani, now rapidly vanishing under lorry-loads of contractors' sand; there is no small island there, but there *is* one in the middle of Bu Dzira ('Rommel's Pool'), and it always looked likely to me – though I never swam there to prove it – that there were the remains of a building on it. As for Monastir, the place which nowadays bears this name lies to the north-east between the Sebkha Selmani and Bu Dzira, and some four miles before one reaches the Coefia 'gardens', while Ain Zeiana ('Blue Lagoon') is a little beyond Coefia to the north, and there is no sign of a 'small hill' or of a stream rising. Goodchild says that an underground stream does discharge into Ain Zeiana, but he does not hazard its source. Where legends are concerned, I believe in plumping for the places with the right 'feel', and for my money 'the wonder' at Coefia and – with an effort of imagination – Jokh el-Kebir are the authentic Gardens of Hesperides and Lethe. Gwyn Williams, who has also delved into these mysteries in *Green Mountain*, seems to agree with me.

There are no legends, so far as I know, about Hagfet er-Rejma, a cave in the first step of the Jebel a few miles beyond Benina. To reach it one simply follows the road to the airport, taking the right fork through Benina village rather than left to the airport itself. This road – a narrow and badly-surfaced one – eventually leads to El Abiar, but to reach the cave one looks out for a quarry ahead and a typically toy-soldier Italian fort on the escarpment to the left of the quarry. The fort stands almost directly above the cave. Just before the quarry, turn left across country: there is a confusion of tracks that are hardly tracks but simply places where cars have been before – aiming, almost certainly, not for the cave but for a deep hole or *howa*, where Libyans, in what Europeans consider to be typically unsporting fashion, blaze away with their shotguns at the pigeons that nest there. It's certainly a pretty pointless occupation, in that no one can ever recover the shot birds since the sides of the hole are far too steep to get down or back again, unless one is lowered on a long rope; and I never saw that happen.

Avoiding the *howa*, anyway, the cave is then clearly in sight, but it has to be reached on foot, walking across the disused railway line from Benghazi to El Merj. From the railway line right up to the cave's entrance you find the reason for coming to this otherwise unpromising spot: a litter of flint implements, largely microliths and scrapers but with some rather more impressive tools if you are lucky. The cave – Hagfet er-Rejma itself – must have been occupied for a longish period into historical times, for I found black-glazed Greek pottery, Roman and Byzantine sherds, and plenty of coarse Arab wares, all very fragmentary, strewn among the flints. The cave was partly excavated in the nineteen-twenties by Italian archaeologists, and some of the flints they found and the plans they made can be seen in the prehistoric section of Tripoli Museum (labelled 'Grotta di el Regima').

Flints seem to me to be at the same time the most beautiful and the most remote of ancient things. To will myself into an

✳ 64

existence in which I can imagine myself fashioning and using these objects is an effort I sometimes make, but never successfully. And yet in their delicate leaf-forms, their entirely natural gradations of colour and patina, their manifestly human working and structure, they seem a composite of the 'poetic' antiquarian artefact. Isolated and labelled like butterflies in museums, they lose their *mana*. I am all for learning about their typology, and I have spent much happy time with one of the few available books which is relevant to the Libyan varieties, McBurney's *The Stone Age of Northern Africa*. Ignorance is not poetry. But the littered slopes below Hagfet er-Rejma are far more evocative than the showcases in Tripoli Museum, and I have almost a miser's feeling of hoarded and unsorted treasure when I spill out one of the tobacco-tins in which I keep these burins and micro-burins, backed-blades and microliths.

If one has several more hours to spare – the journey can be made easily in an hour and a half from Benghazi, but one needs time to wander about – it is good to press on to Asqefar. Between Hagfet er-Rejma and El Abiar there is a tract of desolate scrub and semi-desert on top of the first step of the Jebel, and El Abiar itself has little to detain the traveller. It is an important watering place for goats, sheep, and camels (El Abiar means 'the wells'), and the animals shuffle about in their black and brown and terracotta congregations as you approach the town. There is a secondary school here, with a boarding department that draws on a wide area. Two English friends taught in this school, one of the very few to use English teachers. There is perhaps more sense of a small town, a community, at El Abiar, than one has in most Cyrenaican settlements, but it lacks the charm of Shahat or Derna.

Leaving El Abiar on the only road out – leading eventually to El Merj – you look out for a track on the left about a mile beyond the edge of the town. Follow this for just over six miles, through rising country, green with juniper and myrtle even at the end of a dry summer, with small wadis running to left and right. Modern Asqefar is no more than a white *zawia* with Bedouin tents scattered across the hillside, but the chief interest of the place lies in a cave associated with the Roman-period *gasr*. The *gasr* itself is completely ruinous and confused, the ground covered with the usual litter of sherds and the occasional coin; but the cave, which lies in a hollow at the top of the slope, is one of the strangest and least-visited places in Cyrenaica. Here, in what may have been a sanctuary or a tomb or both – there are ledges cut in the rock which remind one of the necropolis at Cyrene – the walls of the cave have been plastered, painted, and glazed; and shining through the glaze are a series of paintings, some of them concerned with Ulysses and his return from Troy. Most of them are permanently damaged and almost all are disfigured by Arabic scrawls in charcoal, which could easily be removed if someone took the trouble to scrub them with soap and water. But enough comes through to make one stay for a long time, puzzling out the legends and inscriptions. Ulysses tied to the mast, three slim but full-thighed Graces, an opulent Circe whose groin has been hacked away, presumably by some disapproving Muslim – these, together with much lively representation of geese, ducks, horses, and an intertwining pattern of vine-leaves set in dark red squares, show a sophistication which it is hard to reconcile with the simple pastoral scene outside the cave.

A more moving juxtaposition is found on the slope below the cave, where a rusty German helmet sits on top of a branch of dead juniper tree which itself is draped in some thickish tattered cloth that might be all that's left of a Wehrmacht uniform. A shepherd there could tell us nothing but that there had been 'much blood', in some way connected with the caves and shallow depressions which lie all about. Perhaps there was some desperate rearguard action during a retreat from Benghazi: the airports at Benina and Rejma were fiercely fought over several times, according to Alan Moorehead. At any rate, the return from Troy and the retreat from Benghazi here seem to become one, and the battered helmet takes on the remote and talismanic air of some Greek casque. The tents and the goats have nothing to do with either; they are native, resilient, they are what remains.

The road to Tocra, beyond the Coefia gardens and Ain Zeiana, has plenty of interest. Near Driana, which it is tempting – because of the name – to identify with Hadrianopolis, though the site has never been identified, there are two *gsur*: one quite well preserved, opposite the lighthouse before one reaches Driana, and the other just on the other side of the village. There are deep disused rock-cut wells at both, and both *gasr* mounds have been later used as Islamic cemeteries, with the usual cairns of stones and ragged banners. The first of these may possibly be the Gasr el Toweel ('the high tower', as they translate it) of the Beecheys, which they describe as being fifteen miles from Benghazi and four miles from the sea: 'not far from it, also to the eastward, are the lakes described by Edrisi in the neighbourhood of Cafez, separated from the sea by ridges of sand, and running along parallel with the beach. The Arab name of one of them is Zeiana or Aziana. Many ground plans of buildings, chiefly dwelling-houses, may be observed at the distance of about three-quarters of a mile from the lake, which probably occupy the site of that town.' The *gasr* near the lighthouse is more like eighteen miles from Benghazi, and Ain Zeiana is west not east, but certainly there is no trace today of anything like a *gasr* nearer Benghazi on this road, and the primitive foundations and olive-presses one finds near Ain Zeiana are more likely to be Arab than Roman-period.

Richard Goodchild thinks that the ruins at Tansolluk, four miles beyond Driana, are more apt to indicate Hadrianopolis than anything at Driana itself. Here there is a probable Christian church and another building of large masonry, and in the rubble I picked up a base of 'Samian' ware with an unclear potter's stamp. Beyond the two substantial buildings, there stretch away, towards the sea, several acres of strewn stone and potsherds. An air-photograph might show something more definite. If this is really Hadrianopolis, it must have been of much smaller importance than the 'five cities' of the Cyrenaican Pentapolis.

The most spectacular ruin on this road before Tocra is Gasr el Mtanneb, but it is a treacherous place to reach: across rock-strewn ground, thick scrub, and then a *sebkha* which may look firm enough for a vehicle in summer when the water dries but it is best to skirt it gingerly. The first time I visited it, in May, I had difficulty in finding anything like a negotiable track off the main road; so I asked a man in Birsis whether he could point out the way to me. He insisted on getting into the van and accompanying me the whole way, a matter of only a couple of miles but a circuitous journey, using narrow goat tracks between high bunches of scrub, and then driving fast in low gear round the sandy edges of the *ebkha*. Big wind-flecked breakers were rolling in against the dunes, straddling which is Gasr el Mtanneb, the two towers collapsing on to the shore in a heap of masonry over forty feet high. Sand has drifted and piled thickly across the inner and landward walls of the fort, but it must have been a formidable place, perhaps the largest of the bastions built by Justinian for the outer defences of Tocra. Procopius, in his *Buildings*, writes of Justinian's wall at Tocra.

That first visit to the *gasr* ended unfortunately, because when I tried to drive back round the *sebkha* to Birsis with my guide, I found that the van was stuck fast in the sand. To lighten ourselves we unloaded two bits of flotsam the man had asked me to carry back to his hut for him – an empty gas cylinder and a huge beam of wood – but we were still stuck. It took three and a half hours of digging and shoving stones under the wheels to get free, and I felt bad about wasting the time and energy of the Birsis man, who must have been well into his sixties. But he worked hard and un-complainingly. We were both pouring with sweat; and as the van at last heaved and screeched out of the sand we shouted trium-phantly, and we threw our arms round one another as soon as we reached a place where we could safely stop. It took all my urging – in terrible Italian – to persuade him to accept some money from me, for the time I had wasted and the trouble I had caused. He took the whole affair to be the will of Allah, and was only con-cerned that I shouldn't be abandoned and benighted, for it would have been easy enough for him to walk the short distance home.

Birsis, where my companion lived, has a Byzantine church with five arches still standing, a circular *gasr* (or possibly a large cir-cular tomb with a ditch) and a number of other more fragmen-tary buildings of the same period; near by, a mosque, a school, and some small houses have recently been built, next to some older Arab buildings in a state of collapse. Birsis is briefly men-tioned by the early Arab historian Ibn Battuta, as the place where the anchorite Birkius lived – in Islamic lore a sort of St An-thony figure, tempted by a girl but resisting her through the grace of God. It is also the site of the *marabout* of Sidi Mohammed Bu Zuetina, who is said to have planted his stick in the ground there one night, and woke up to discover that it had changed into a huge olive tree; but though there are olive trees quite close by, none of those there now seems big enough to be legendary. Shrines

✳ 68

like this are still visited annually so that the saint's memory can be commemorated with a festive meal and sometimes with games, such as feats on horseback.

In the ditch or moat surrounding the circular ruin I came upon a slab of stone with a Greek inscription, hidden among the heaps of other stones. A man was hoeing tomato plants in a small fertile patch of red earth, the earth fed with water from one of the two very deep and obviously old rock-cut wells. He was loudly singing to himself – a kind of liturgical shout or *Songsprach* – when I approached him and asked his permission to carry the inscription away in the van, so that I could hand it over to the Antiquities Department. He seemed a bit puzzled, as well he might, that I wanted a bit of stone, though he gave me permission straight away. He nodded sagely but I think without understanding when I tried to explain that it was 'old Greek writing' (it turned out, in fact, to be part of a Byzantine tombstone, and all that was decipherable was the word KYPIOU – 'to the Lord'). In this he was unlike the youths who came up to me one day when I was picking up surface flints on the barren and dusty plain near Coefia; when I told them what I was doing and what these bits of stone were, they obviously thought I was mad, though they were too polite to show it. Sensing this, I finished my halting explanation by simply pointing at my head and saying '*Majnoon*' ('mad'). This made them roar with laughter and they immediately shook hands very warmly and clapped me on the back. All foreigners are mad, but some are mad in more interesting ways than others.

Tocra, seven miles on from Birsis, is the Greek Tauchira, and the closest companion to Benghazi of the Cyrenaican Pentapolis. The Beecheys visited it and made a plan of the ancient town which is still reliable and has never been replaced, though a surveying party from Newcastle University has recently been at work there. It was the happy hunting ground of George Dennis, the nineteenth-century British consul at Benghazi, a man whom I sometimes rather guiltily thought of as my antiquarian ancestor. Dennis was an indefatigable searcher, rifling tombs in Benghazi, and digging up (or causing to be dug up) large tracts of Cyrene, Apollonia and Ptolemais, all of which he found 'disappointing' – the loot was not grand enough. He had no interest in scientific archaeology but a strong lust for possession. At Tocra he proved to be luckier than elsewhere, acquiring from the local people some fine pottery, including the huge Panathenaic vases which are now in the British Museum.

The ruins are approached through the modern village of Tocra, which is little more than a group of low whitewashed houses and shops round a quadrangle. A couple of hundred yards away, on the sea, is the Turco-Italian fort, built in ludicrously theatrical fashion: as one drives towards it, it seems like some child's cardboard cut-out outlined against the brilliant blue sky. It now houses the offices and museum run by the local representative of the Antiquities Department, Ali Salaam. Ali Salaam is locally known as Ali Lectric; his strange but not entirely un-Arabic-sounding surname coming from the fact that his grandfather was the first man in the district to know how to put in wiring and the like. 'El Lectric' has an authentic ring to me, though I am told that true Arabic would eschew the cluster of consonants in the middle.

Ali Salaam is an example of Libyanization working in an unorthodox but entirely successful way. He comes from the Shahat district – the modern village on the Cyrene site – and from his schooldays he took a much closer interest than the other boys in the excavations going on there. He began work as a labourer on such excavations, but his interest and intelligence were soon obvious and he was given a number of supervisory chores. Richard Goodchild took him under his wing, and eventually – while he was still in his twenties – he was given the job of Antiquities Inspector, Tocra Area. For most of 1966 he was sent to Tripoli to do a comprehensive archaeological course at the Castello Museum, but this is the only formal training he has ever had. Yet he is an observant and knowledgeable archaeologist, and it was due to him that a number of interested foreigners, including myself, were given the chance to do some official digging at Tocra.

The job assigned us was to excavate one end of the barracks of the Byzantine period; or rather, one room in a problematical area of the barracks which might be late Byzantine or perhaps very early Arab – this was for us to reveal. But before we began work, we were invited one Friday afternoon to go out to Tocra and be introduced by Ali Salaam to the local head-men: the *mudir*, the chief of police, and so on. A little ceremony was organized inside the fort. We sat on benches and were welcomed, while we drank glasses of tea and ate cakes. Everybody made a speech, and we were taken on a tour of the site. All this was to ensure that we were properly accepted by the people of Tocra, for the majority of men there are employed as labourers and *ghaffirs* by the Antiquities Department, and strangers ferreting about were not encouraged. Nevertheless, I enjoyed some innocuous plunderings, in no way connected with the official dig. In the crumbling cliff-face west of the fort, a friend and I found a complete Byzantine lamp, a number of debased late-Roman coins, and much pottery, some of it delicately fine, such as the well-curved handle of a Greek black-glazed *kylix*. And when my parents visited us, my father found in the same cliff a small terracotta figurine of Nike, Victory, complete but for the head. It was a little farther to the east that erosion by sea and wind revealed an important presumed hoard of votive pottery which was properly excavated in 1964–5 by the British School at Athens under John Boardman: 900 Archaic vases, of the period 630–550 B.C., which proved that Tocra was just as early a foundation as Cyrene, rather than a later development, which is what Herodotus seems to suggest. It is not known whether the building in which this vast hoard was found was a temple shrine or a merchant's warehouse, but the inscriptions on the pottery seem mainly to be votive. They are ranged in the temporary museum at Tocra on long wooden shelves, and one of the most remarkable things about them to the layman is their fine state of preservation: many of them are completely undamaged.

'The room at Tocra' – the minor 'official' dig in which I took part – was not of this calibre. In fact it was disagreeably reminiscent, except for the setting and the weather, of those depressing digs in England where at the end of a month all that has turned up is an ambiguous streak of ash in the trench, or one scrap of (?) Middle Bronze Age (?) pottery. Negative evidence, of course, is supposed to be meat and drink to the professional, but it is cold comfort to the amateur. Three months of week-end work revealed nothing but basketsful of coarse pottery, unhelpful because of the difficulty of distinguishing between late Byzantine and early Arab wares, and eventually a coarsely pebbled floor. One loom-weight, decorated with a stamp that might represent Mercury tying on his sandals, a man removing a thorn from his foot, or an athlete with cramp, was the only other artefact. And even our technique was not impeccable. My favourite cringing memory of the whole business is of the afternoon when we had reached floor level and Dick – who came for the exercise and the company – suddenly said, while my back was turned, 'Anthony, there's a very soft feel to all this stuff.' It turned out that he had put his pick through the pebble floor and was wrenching it out in great pink gouts, like an inexpert dentist excavating a recalcitrant tooth. Anyway, having cleared our room, swept it up tidily, measured it, and handed back our tools, we were on the whole glad to have done with it. Those who came in the early stages expecting Tutankhamen in the first spadeful had soon dropped away, but even the veterans were disenchanted.

Yet such trivia can't obscure the imaginative impact of Tocra: one of the last Byzantine fortresses in Cyrenaica, within whose walls the Governor of the Pentapolis retired with his troops to make a last stand, and where the early Roman-period gymnasium is surrounded by the stones carved by the *ephebes* – the young citizens of eighteen or twenty who had been conscripted for garrison duty, and who commemorated on these stones in Greek their names and their achievements. *Graffiti*, whether in lavatories or elsewhere, are always interesting, sometimes funny, sometimes poignant; and those at Tocra, carved in their diversity of styles – some crude and hasty, some done with great deliberation and skill – are the most moving I know. The Byzantine wall of Tocra, Justinian's wall, is still impressively high in many places, running through groves of palms; and looking westward to Gasr el Mtanneb or south to the sharply-rising brown ridge of the Jebel one can get some sense of the vulnerability of this town which, in one fashion or another, lasted for over 1,400 years. It lies in the plain like a prize to be captured: harbourless, consumed gradually by the sea on one side, and swept by the blustery coastal winds.

The coast road from Tocra eastwards is the easiest approach to Tolmeita, but though it is a new road the surface is rapidly degenerating, with bone-shaking craters forming wherever the many conduits run under it. Ruined buildings – fortified farmhouses – flank it on both sides, and it passes by Jedida, one of the few village-centres in Libya which the Italians built specifically for the Libyans. This was not an act of altruistic kindness, since those who were intended to live there were the dispossessed herdsmen and small farmers of the Barce plain. In any case, the houses were never inhabited, because by the time they were under construction in 1942 the armies were ranging across the land, and permanent settlement was an even less attractive notion to Cyrenaicans in those conditions than it is now. Today, only one of the fifty Italian-built farmhouses is lived in, and that because the owner is so poor that he cannot afford a tent. In the middle of the settlement is a large square, surrounded by the unfinished public buildings of Jedida, abandoned almost thirty years ago and crumbling into the dusty plain of Bu Trab.

The first glimpses of Tolmeita when approached from this direction are of the Tauchira gate, which does not connect with the modern road, and of the huge Hellenistic tower-tomb, placed high on a cube of solid rock jutting up in isolation above the city's largest ancient quarry: the building stone has been hacked away to leave it free on its pinnacle. The tomb stands over forty feet high, a pink monolith, and was constructed for multiple burial; but no one is clear for whom. The local tradition is that it is the 'Tomb of Pharaoh', and though that sounds at first no more likely than the sort of mound English villagers assure you is 'Caesar's Camp', archaeologists have at least not dismissed the name lightly; because although 'Pharaoh' is fanciful, 'Ptolemy' would not be, and there are close connections – the town's name itself, for a start – between Ptolemais and the ruling family of Hellenistic Cyrenaica. Whoever it was intended for, its size and its beleaguered isolation single it out, the biggest tomb in a land riddled and strewn with tombs.

Modern Tolmeita is partly surrounded by an Italian wall which can never have been meant to be defensive, but rather one of those pathetic theatrical gestures the Italian military administrators apparently loved to go in for. The village itself has a depressed air, a single street with crumbling one-storey shops and houses facing one another. Very few settlements in Cyrenaica have much feeling of purpose (Shahat and Jaghbub, for quite different reasons, are exceptions), and one can account for this in the case of Tolimeta when one realizes that it stands below the rich Barce plain and has no significant agriculture of its own. The low rainfall on the coast allows only dry farming and grazing, and even the wells along this stretch are in peril, because they too easily choke with clay after the winter inundation through the wadis which sweep so precipitously down from the Jebel. The harbour, which must have been considerable in ancient times when Ptolemais was the port of Barca, is largely silted up, ruinous, and little used. As at Tocra, Shahat and Sousa, a large part of the adult male population is employed by the Department of Antiquities, as labourers and *ghaffirs*, so that for most of the year (except when a foreign archaeological expedition needs pick-and-shovel men) the village is full of quasi-antiquarian layabouts.

The most ubiquitous of these is in fact an ex-employee of the Department, for he was sacked some years ago for carrying on a trade which his dismissal has done nothing to stop. This is Mohammed. I never discovered his full name, but somehow I attached to him the name 'Ali ben Shufti', and it stuck: 'shufti' being, of course, the British army corruption of the Arabic 'nshuff' (look). He is a short, round, battered, genial man of about forty, who generally wears a shapeless Harris tweed jacket and a pair of the characteristic full-bottomed pantaloons (the seat-flap hangs down like a disgraced codpiece) which are so common in Cyrenaica. Out of these he produces small bags, tins, twists of rag and paper, in which nestle the only desirable antiquities you are likely to see for sale in Libya. At Leptis, Sabratha and Tocra one may be approached by small boys with a few coins; in Cyrene the presence of the Department's headquarters seems to have effectively squashed even that harmless trade; while at Apollonia the most persistent merchant is as likely to offer a plastic doll's head or a handful of nineteenth-century Papal *lire* as anything else.

But Ali ben Shufti is in his way a bit of a connoisseur. He has kept his ears open when the experts (self-styled or genuine) have theorized over his offerings, and he hesitantly trots out 'Greek', 'Roman', 'Byzantine', as he fetches forth his goods. He is open to bargaining but his prices are not on the whole cheap and he is no fool. It always surprised me that he had been dismissed from the Department, because the sort of stray finds he scratches out of the top-soil and picks up on the surface are not of much precise archaeological interest, though covetable enough as antiquarian objects: good coins of all ancient periods (sometimes silver, never gold), heads of Tanagra-type figurines, small pots and lamps, coloured glass beads, a few semi-precious gem-stones from rings, fragments of decorative bronzes, and the like. He must have made a fortune a few years ago when Chicago University launched a series of expeditions into Tolmeita, which resulted in a certain amount of excavation, handsomely recorded in a massive volume* a concomitant of which was 'Finds Locally Purchased', including 173 coins. Thus whenever one haggled with Ali ben Shufti, or havered over a price, his ready reply was always, 'But the Americans – they will give me £10', or whatever large multiple seemed appropriate to the deal. He beamed and chortled, and usually got his way – with me, and with others who sometimes paid him absurd prices.

In Libya, unlike Italy, Greece, Egypt and the Levant, one can be pretty certain generally that whatever is offered is not a fake: it may be a bit of rubbish (like the Apollonia doll's head, which was obviously produced in good faith through sheer ignorance), but Libya has not yet developed a curio trade, and presumably won't do so until the tourists start arriving in substantial quantities. Occasionally a dubious coin somehow gets into circulation; and I once picked up off the ground in the ruined Cathedral at Cyrene a tiny limestone bearded head which looked suspiciously like the product of some Shahat schoolboy's idle half-hour, though one can't be certain. But neither the depressing 'replicas' of Athens's Monastiraki or Cairo's Khan el-Khalil, nor the cunningly patinated fakes of more sophisticated craftsmen, have taken over in Libya.

Antiquarian acquisitiveness apart, Tolmeita is a delightful site, especially in spring when the usually arid plain proliferates with blue, red, yellow and purple flowers right up to the foothills of the Jebel. Goats browse in the Palace of Anastasius, a tiny owl blinks and shifts from foot to foot on top of a column, and the lie of the land is such that one stumbles on forts, cisterns, theatres and arches almost without warning, rather than seeing them all from an Olympian height as one does at Cyrene. Like Euhesperides, Tauchira and Apollonia, it was a city of the plain and the sea. Its most distinguished resident was Synesius, its bishop of the early fifth century A.D., who has been of such importance to me that I

* *Ptolemais: City of the Libyan Pentapolis*, by Carl H. Kraeling, Chicago University Press, 1962.

✳ 75

must leave him for another chapter. But it is proper here to say that the so-called 'Headquarters of the Dux', the walls of which still stand in places to a height of fifteen feet, is the very spot where Synesius must often have had his acid and angry exchanges with the military governors of the area, chief among them Andronicus. It is a pity that archaeological evidence seems to reject the notion that Ptolemais's one certain church, the Fortress Church to the west of the city, was the one where Synesius officiated.

The three most interesting survivals at Ptolemais are the Square of the Cisterns, the Palace of the Columns, and the Odeon. The first is a large agora-like area under which lie nine great chambers, together making an impressive water cistern. As in every Cyrenaican site with the exception of Cyrene itself, water at Ptolemais was always a great problem, and much energy and skill was put into the digging of wells, the building of aqueducts, and the construction of cisterns. In the Square of the Cisterns you can go down the steps on the south-eastern side and walk through the semi-circular vaults, with just enough light coming through the small shafts cut in the roof to allow you to move about easily. The Palace of the Columns is a rather grandiose name ('Il Palazzo delle Colonne' was the invention of the Italian archaeologist Pesce) for the large villa which stands almost in the middle of the excavated parts of Ptolemais. Here there are baths, mosaics, and fragments of bright wall-plaster in deep red, apple-green and yellow. The Odeon is a small theatre which it is supposed might have been used for aquatic displays, since the remains of a large water-tank is the central feature, though it is now hard to imagine in this ruinous setting the erotic performances which tempted out the citizens of Ptolemais.

The road out of Tolmeita up the Jebel and on to the Barce plain is one of the worst-surfaced in Cyrenaica, but it is worth it for the view as you wind up the narrow pass through the hills, between junipers, pines and myrtles, with steep wadis descending to the plain. This road brings you out on the main north road five miles east of Barce. The run in is across some of the richest farmland in Libya: a great, flat, fertile disk, green and lush, dotted with the 1,800 houses of the former Italian settlers, some rehabilitated by the Libyan government, others smashed by the war or simply crumbling away into the plain through neglect. This Barce plain is more influenced in its aspect by the weather than any other part of Libya I have seen: for in steady summer weather when the sky is blue it looks like a calm green sea, benevolent and rich, but clouds and rain turn it into something as bleak and wild as Bodmin Moor.

The town of Barce (more properly, El Merj: Barce is the Italian version of the ancient *Barca*, which is still the name the Arabs use for the whole province of Cyrenaica) was largely destroyed by the earthquake of February 1963, when 300 people were killed and thousands were made homeless. The solider Italian buildings survived more or less intact, but the small houses and shops made of rubble collapsed instantly, crushing whoever was inside. Barce before the earthquake must have been a pleasant place, sitting as it does in the middle of its fruitful plain. The new town to the north, now under construction by a Polish company, seems likely to be grander but a great deal more antiseptic in its atmosphere: severe modern blocks of flats, regimented bungalows, wide dual carriageways launching themselves off into nothing. I wonder who precisely will live there. Those who were made homeless by the earthquake have been housed for the past few years in a shanty town of wood and sheet-metal hutments up against the foothills of the Jebel south of the town, where even the neat temporary schools provided by earthquake relief have had their large windows painted over, so that no one can look out – or in. An Arab building looks in on itself, and the extrovert architecture of the new Barce is not likely to appeal to a people as deeply traditional as this.

From Barce you can take the southern road which climbs the second step of the Jebel. Seven miles along this there is a turning to the right, a narrow road but well-surfaced, which runs south to Jerdis el Abid, a distance of fifteen miles. Along it are strung a series of Roman fortified farms, which command most of the high points to left and right. In the valley between are the usual Italian farmhouses, but these thin out towards Jerdis el Abid, and tracks run off now and then to the right which lead down into the desert – to Msus, for example. Aiming one day for Gasr Jeballa, the most spectacular of the ruins and more like a permanent military fort than a fortified farmhouse, we took the wrong track by mistake, and though I soon realized what I had done I decided to press on to see where it might get to. Gradually the cultivated land gives way to an undulating plain covered with scrub, an empty landscape where the smallest thing – a cairn of stones, an abandoned plough – attracts to itself an attention one would never normally give. An eagle hovered overhead. Two gazelles, their white scuts flashing in the sunlight, scampered away to the west. And at the top of a slight rise we came across an abandoned Bedouin encampment, with the rings of small stones marking where the tents had been pitched. Close by were the cairns of the dead, and a litter of rusty sickles, battered tin bowls, old jerry-cans for water, scatters of grain, rags of bright *barracans*. Apart from the patches of greyish-green camelthorn, there was not a living thing in sight. I realized that it would be mad to press on further without bigger reserves of petrol than we had, so we slept the night there and turned back in the morning. On the way to the Jerdis el Abid road we met a couple of herdsmen and asked them where the track we had given up eventually led to. 'Msus,' they said, and the word seemed like a rebuke; for at Msus one is in the 'real' desert, and to have got there by following my original impulse would have been to have met a challenge – a challenge which I funked.

Still, Gasr Jeballa is a fit enough place to aim for, and is worth several visits. It stands on a hill to the right of the narrow road to Jerdis el Abid, a mile down a rough track which is safe enough for a car in dry weather. Its massive walls and arches overtop heaps of huge masonry, on some of which are inscriptions in Greek and Libyan. On one fallen block is a much-worn carving of men on horseback. Trudging up the steep slope one day I found a bronze sestertius of Gordian III, clear and legible but with a chunk neatly cut out of the edge, presumably so that the coin would be of a lower denomination than that originally intended.

Another day I arrived with the children and was looking round the site when a shepherd came up and got into conversation. He said that he often found old coins lying about there, and asked us to visit his tent, which was pitched in a sheltered place below the *gasr*. From a distance, a Bedouin tent seems low and constricting, but inside we found that the two roof-poles (hewn logs) were well over six feet high, and our host's father, who was a tall man, could easily move about without bending. We were offered cushions set against the rolled blankets and bedding at one end of the tent, and while the inevitable tea was being brewed we were given *leben* (buttermilk) and then – when the children showed, with unusual politeness, that it was not to their taste – fresh goat's milk, warm from the udders of the goat we could see tethered outside. All round the tent were water containers of all kinds – leather bags, dried skins, buckets and jerry-cans – and I realized again how basic to Bedouin life is the finding and storing of good water. The floor was simply trodden earth, but it was kept scrupulously clean and dry, and the whole arrangement and order of the tent made our urban clutter seem gross and excessive.

Pinned to the top of one of the roof-poles were two torn pages from the Koran, which we were proudly shown. But on the whole we were not busied with attentions but entertained with food and drink and left to watch the family go about its usual business. The man's wife – unveiled, as is customary among countrywomen, unlike the shrouded and secretive women of the towns – was spinning wool on a wooden distaff, while the grandfather and an uncle played with the two little boys, whose only toys seemed to be old torch-batteries tied with pieces of string, which they towed about. After the third round of glasses of tea, when it is proper for guests to leave, the man fished out of a bag and gave to me an early Islamic coin, with the Star of David on one side, small, worn and rubbed. He led us out from the shade of the tent into the bright sunlight, and left us at a point by the *gasr* where some of his neighbours were threshing corn, driving two horses in a circle with a beam dragged behind, while men winnowed the grain by hurling it into the air and letting the wind blow away the chaff.

It is easy for the urban Westerner to sentimentalize the simplicity, courtesy and generosity of the Bedouin, but it is hard not to be impressed and moved by them nevertheless. The Cyrenaican Bedouin is not an emotional, demonstrative, or ingratiating man, but he has a straightforward dignity which is far more appealing. Much has been made of the fact that the Arabic words for *stranger* and *guest* are the same, and a visitor to the hotels of Benghazi and Tripoli may feel inclined to sneer at the collocation and to think it out of date. But at Gasr Jeballa that day we were made to feel its truth.

✳ 79

5 Tripoli and the West

ON a Saturday or Sunday evening, walking down the main boulevard of Tripoli, Sharia Istiklal, which runs from the Cathedral to the Castello, you might be in an Italian city. As nightfall comes, it's like a changing of the guard – Italian for Arab. Young men and women parade up and down, or chat in groups, whistling or calling out to their friends who ride by in cars or on motor-bikes. The clothes and the gestures are from Milan, Florence, Naples, Rome. There is hardly a Libyan on the streets, and the pavement cafés are full of Italian farmers in from the country, dressed in their best suits, sipping camparis and cinzanos.

Everywhere the Italian element remains strong in Tripoli; in Tripolitania there are estimated to be almost 30,000 Italians, most of them living in or close to Tripoli itself. Shop signs, restaurants, and newspapers proclaim their presence: the *Giornale di Tripoli* was founded in 1923 and still continues. There are two or three good bookshops, run by Italians: I remember noticing in the window of one of them a copy of *Colpisci a morte il padre*, romanzo di John Wain. And whereas in Benghazi almost every overt trace of the Italian colonization has been obliterated, in Tripoli even such a thing as the commemorative plaque put up by Count Volpi over the old Turkish city wall at Bab el Jedida has been allowed to remain. In the Museum's epigraphy section, an imaginative idea – but one hard to imagine in Benghazi – has been to display, at the end of a long series of Punic, Roman, Byzantine and Islamic inscriptions, a selection of Italian monuments: memorials to soldiers killed in the first and second Senussi wars, *graffiti* scratched by troops in remote garrisons, grandiose plaques commemorating Volpi, Balbo, King Victor Emmanuel and Mussolini. One of the few memorials not to survive was the immense statue of Mussolini which used to stand on a plinth at the foot of the Castello walls, looking up Sharia Istiklal (formerly the Corso Vittorio Emmanuele): the plinth remains, and when I bought a postcard of the Castello in 1950 one could see on it how the outline of the statue still remained on the photograph, a ghostly presence defying the developer's chemicals.

It was from the roof of the Castello that in May 1951 I saw the triumphal entry into Tripoli of Idris, who had just been proclaimed King of the new Libya, though in fact it was not until December 24th, 1951, that Libya was formally created as an independent kingdom – the first state to be 'founded' by the United Nations. Idris is a Cyrenaican, and, more than that, the leader of the Senussi Brotherhood, the nineteenth-century Muslim puritan sect which evangelized North Africa: Idris's grandfather was the founder of the sect, and he lies buried in the chief Senussi shrine at Jaghbub. The Senussi persuasion never really took root in Tripolitania, and in the years before and after independence there were many Tripolitanians who resented the idea of a united Libyan kingdom under Idris. A Tripolitanian nationalist party was founded which wanted the western province to be a separate republic: Cyrenaicans might do what they wished about having a kingdom of their own, but many Tripolitanians, with their greater Western sophistication, their lack of religious fervour, their comparative lack of reliance on hierarchical tribal notions, their richer agriculture, felt themselves to be distinct from their more primitive Eastern neighbours; and some of the more extreme members were prepared to use force to keep that distinction.

So it was that Idris's triumphal entry was marred by an incident that gave me my first experience of mass political violence. As the Senussi sheikhs proudly rode by on their horses, coming down what is now Sharia Omar Mukhtar to turn the corner below the Castello which leads into Sharia Istiklal, the crowds surged forward to see Idris follow them in a big closed Daimler. Just below the Castello, there was a flash and an explosion in the street not far in front of the royal car; someone in the crowd had thrown a 'red devil' grenade. Immediately the police who were lining the route turned on the crowd behind them and waded into them with their batons raised above their heads, and people fell on to the pavements like skittles. Even from where I was standing, high above the street, I could see the blood, and hear the great wail and screaming from the crowd, the shouting of the police, and could see the horses rear and scatter as the sheikhs and mounted policemen tried to keep them under control. Then there was another explosion, which seemed to come from within the crowd itself, and the police pressed on until there were thousands of people pushed down to the jetty which stands by the sea below the columns bearing the Italian statues of Romulus and Remus and the Lion of St Mark. Idris's car moved slowly on and out of sight, with those who had fainted or been wounded still lying on the pavement and in the street.

It was not an auspicious entry into the largest city of his new kingdom, but within a few years all political parties had been abolished and any coherent opposition had been crushed. There were gaolings and exiles, the closing down of those 'cultural clubs' which had in so many cases been the innocuous fronts for militant organizations, and the newspapers and magazines they published were banned. There are still whispers of Tripolitanian disaffection, but the idea that the province could stand on its own without Cyrenaica was pretty effectively swept away by the discovery of oil in the late nineteen-fifties. It soon became clear that the richest oil-strikes were in Cyrenaica, including the first important and still the most productive one: Zelten. Tripolitania might have a better organized rural economy, but it could not compete financially with the far more lucrative petroleum industry. And Idris has been politically careful in his choice of Prime Ministers, usually alternating one from Cyrenaica with one from Tripolitania; there has even been one from the Fezzan, which in the pre-1963 tripartite structure of Libya was never, and could never be, on a par with the other two.

The old city of Tripoli stretches away behind the Castello, beginning with the *souks* or market-alleyways, which are less impressive than those in Cairo and Tunis but have considerably more interest than Benghazi's. Here there are metalworkers, beating out copper and brass trays, making jewellery out of gold, silver, and semi-precious stones; rugs from Misurata (though many are imported from Tunisia, Morocco, Pakistan and India, and some of the most 'oriental' in fact come from Belgium, of all places); basketwork and woven rushwork from Tauorga; pottery from Tarhuna and Kussabat. Sheepskins, camel saddles, *magruna* (shepherds' pipes made from bamboo with rams' horns), just about complete the local products made and sold here.

The European consulates used to be in this part of Tripoli, founded in the early nineteenth century when Britain, France and Italy began to take an interest in the Barbary Coast trade. The old French and British consulates are now tenements, though one can see how solid and grand they must have been, and there has been some attempt to save them from demolition. But the idea of 'preservation societies' is quite alien to Libyans, who automatically equate the old – in the material world, anyway – with the primitive and the out-of-date.

Hemmed round by a clutter of Turkish and modern buildings on the seafront in the north of the old city is the oldest surviving building in Tripoli: the Arch of Marcus Aurelius. It stands in a hollow open square below the modern street level, a four-sided arch which originally stood at a cross-roads. It is built throughout of white Greek marble, and although some of the sculptural decoration (Minerva and Apollo driving chariots drawn by sphinxes and winged griffins; portrait medallions and winged victories) is missing, on the whole it is in an extraordinarily good state of preservation – especially when one thinks of the vicissitudes it must have suffered through the centuries. When the Italians occupied Tripoli in 1911, it was found to have been transformed into a cinema.

Close by are Tripoli's few old mosques, including the Gurgi, the Osman Pasha (in a simple courtyard, with small private houses placed round it, the whole giving the atmosphere of a cloistered retreat away from the noise of the *souk* area), and the most elaborate one, the Ahmed Pasha Karamanli, built in the eighteenth century by the Karamanli family, who for a period of about one hundred and fifty years were effectively the rulers of Tripoli under the remote supervision of the Sublime Porte. But even the Karamanli Mosque cannot measure up to the great mosques of Cairo, and indeed Libya as a whole is not a country of distinguished Islamic architecture. The fine tiles which line the interior of the Karamanli were imported from Italy, and only the rich stone carvings, like solid fretwork, seem native. Mosques are not simply places of prayer; an important secondary function is to act as hostels for pilgrims, and on one visit to the Karamanli I saw a

✳ 83

party of Algerian pilgrims from Constantine, presumably on their way back after going on *Haj* to Mecca. They were sitting on mats in an inner courtyard, writing letters, talking and sleeping.

The huge city walls which partly encircle the old city were built by the Turks in 1530. The most impressive view of them is near the Bab el Jedida ('the new gate'), close to the bus-station, the State Tobacco Factory, and Tripoli's rather poor version of a flea-market – second-hand bedsteads, old clothes, and sanitary fittings which look as if they would be better off on a scrap heap. Following the walls round to the Castello, you come to the fish-market, which is having new quarters built on the waterfront near the Arch of Marcus Aurelius. I was told by one of my students whose family had a business on the waterfront that about eighty per cent of the fishing is done by Libyans and only twenty per cent by foreigners – mainly Maltese and Italians. If this is so it is a very different situation from Benghazi, where the fishing is almost entirely monopolized by Greeks and Cretans. Fish is not a usual part of Libyan diet, and most of the catches go to the foreign-patronized restaurants.

Unlike Benghazi, it's possible to eat well in Tripoli, but I would hesitate to recommend any place as serving particularly notable local dishes. It is better to stick to Greek or Italian. The Acropole, in the Cathedral square, is a clean, appetizing, perhaps rather colourless restaurant, where the atmosphere is not noticeably Greek, despite the management and the waiters. A better bet is the Romagna, in an arcade (built, like most of Tripoli's arcades, on a quasi-Roman plan) between Sharia Istiklal and Sharia 24 Decembre. This is the restaurant most patronized by Italians both from the city itself and from the farms round about, and it feels very much like a decent Italian *trattoria*. Tripolitania's wine, like Cyrenaica's, is fair to good. When I was in Tripoli in 1950 and 1951, the wine-making was in the hands of a native Jewish family, the Nahums: Harry Scammell and I had a theory that the label contained a clue to the quality of the wine, a clue that the customer was not intended to know about. We had noticed that some bottles had a small dot, some a large dot, and some no dot at all. We came to the conclusion that the dotless bottles were the best of all, though all cost the same price. Unfortunately we never put this fanciful theory to the test by sending back large-dotted bottles. Nowadays the wine is made by Greeks (as in Cyrenaica), and there are no dots on the labels.

The British army stayed on in Tripolitania, in diminishing numbers, until March 1966, when the last barracks were handed over to the Libyan army, together with the British Military Hospital and the Forces Broadcasting Station. Now it is as if they have never been, except for the odd barber who has left up an IN BOUNDS sign, and the fading OUT OF BOUNDS notices in some parts of the *souk*. There is still a considerable British element among Tripoli's foreigners (oil people, business representatives, diplomats, teachers, and so forth), but the tone is set by the Italians – though through the accident of occupation the British managed to acquire the most imposing site for the British Embassy, down on what was the Lungomare and is now Sharia Adrian Pelt, and close by it is one of the most attractive private houses in the city: now a British Embassy residence, it is a villa of the Turkish period with a big veranda overlooking the sea, and a garden with fountains and spouting gargoyles.

The 'Garden City' of Tripoli, which was largely taken over by the British for offices, clubs and living quarters during the time of the military administration, is now almost entirely lived in by senior Libyan government officials and some Italians: a quarter of large shady villas and gardens lying behind the Cathedral and round the King's palace, which was formerly the Italian governor's residence. Most foreigners now live in a suburb on the Sabratha road to the west, Giorgimpopoli. This is a hideous monument to private enterprise, each villa garishly coloured in pinks or greens or reds or purples, some of them bizarrely shaped in the extreme. The supermarkets and hairdressers are like a crazy approximation to someone's dream of America the Golden, a PX world. Benghazi's equivalent, Fueihat, seems chaste and restrained in comparison. The best way of catching the flavour of Giorgimpopoli without actually going there was to read the English-language weekly newspaper, the *Sunday Ghibli*, which was founded by Cedric Johnston, an Englishman, soon after the military administration began. To read Pike Tilbury's 'Sunday Table Talk' column in the *Sunday Ghibli*, one would have thought Tripoli's social life was one long whirl of gaiety, until one began to

✳ 85

notice that the same names of diplomats, airline executives and 'publicists' recurred with monotonous regularity. It was, at any rate a brave attempt to make expatriates feel that Tripoli was as swinging as the cities from which they had been temporarily exiled. (The paper was forced to close in 1967, in circumstances I explained on page 58.)

Sabratha, the third of the three Phoenician-Roman cities of Tripolitania, is forty miles along the road west of Giorgimpopoli. Along this stretch, and inland, is the stronghold of the Berber element still remaining in Libya: Zavia, Sorman, Zuara, Zanzur and Agelat. In Zuara those who consider themselves to be Berbers form almost half the population, and they are a considerable minority in the other villages. But it is often difficult to draw a firm line between them and the Arabs, for they all speak Arabic, follow Islam, and physically often have the same features as Arabs. Yet Berber is still commonly spoken as the language within the family, and there is a tendency towards fairer hair, lighter colouring and blue eyes. The origins of the Berbers are obscure. The early Arab historian el-Bekri identifies them with the defeated Philistines, and other early Arab writers, such as Ibn Khaldun, even state categorically that Goliath was the ancestor of all the indigenous North Africans.

One of my best students was a Berber from Sorman, and he was intensely proud of it, as well as being eager to make linguistic sense of 'his' language; he had tried, without success, to get hold of some of the few studies which have been made of Berber, all by French scholars, because to him it was simply a spoken language and he wanted to learn the alphabet and formal grammar.

The landscape between Zavia and Sabratha is well cultivated and keeps its Italian quality much more than anywhere in Cyrenaica: just as the Jebel Akhdar must have appealed to the early Greek settlers because it looks very Greek, so Tripolitania was turned by the Italians into a fourth shore of Italy: olive trees set in their trim plots, cypresses along the roadside and lining the way up to the farmhouses, the neat, well-kept little churches. The most obvious signs of Arab occupation are huts made of palm leaves, quite solid and not shack-like, of a kind different from anywhere else in Libya. Otherwise it is a landscape almost entirely laid out by the pre-war Italian colonists, and kept that way.

At Sabratha there's a walk of just under a mile from the main road to the ruins, and there isn't the sudden feeling of revelation that one gets at Leptis, descending suddenly from the modern to the ancient level: from a long way off the city begins to come into focus, and much less of it stands above ground or has been excavated than at Leptis. Sabratha's chief glory is its theatre, which was one of the Italian archaeologists' most ambitious and most successful efforts in restoration. One can see in the Castello Museum in Tripoli a large scale-model showing it complete, and the Italians made a very close approximation to this. The huge *scaenae frons*, a back-curtain of masonry, towers up with three colonnaded storeys, and through its entrances can be seen more columns, more walls, with the Mediterranean breaking blue and white beyond, a narrow shaft between white and golden columns. I have seen it in bright sunshine, and also in unusual wind and rain in April, when it truly seemed a theatre of the elements. Today there is an annual Sabratha Festival, when the theatre is used for plays and operas, and among all the talk about tourism this seems to be one idea which is not only good but has actually been put into practice.

Apart from the theatre and the museum, which is bigger and better-stocked than that at Leptis (though still maddening in its lack of information, without labels or catalogues), the only other possession which can surpass Leptis's is the magnificent mosaic from Justinian's Basilica: Procopius mentioned the Basilica in his *Buildings,* and though little is left of the church itself the mosaic has been preserved in one wing of the museum, where it can be seen from above by climbing a viewing-stand. Caught in the swirls of a great Tree of Paradise, peacocks and all manner of birds peck and fly among an intricate pattern of leaves, flowers, and bunches of grapes. Its only equal among the many rich mosaics of Libya is that from Gasr Lebia in Cyrenaica, which is of the same period – that final flowering under Justinian before the anarchy of the seventh century and afterwards.

West of Sabratha, the coast road to Tunisia runs through country which gradually loses its Italianate quality and becomes bleak and barren until well beyond the frontier, at Gabes, where I stayed in December 1950 and saw the French conscripts sitting about in the town square, almost suffocated with *cafard.* If one is not going into Tunisia, the main interest lies far to the south-west, where the oasis of Ghadames was the chief posting-station on the Roman caravan-route from the gold, ivory, peacocks and apes of equatorial Africa to the port of Sabratha. But although the proper way to approach Ghadames authentically should no doubt be by camel along some southward track, or at least by car along the rough unsurfaced road via Giado and Nalut, I arrived there in 1967 by air, in one of the three planes a week from Tripoli, and took only an hour and twenty minutes on the journey. This has been one of the services started recently by Kingdom of Libya Airlines, no doubt primarily as a tourist incentive, but on my flight there and back I was the only passenger going there for pleasure: the others were all people who lived in Ghadames and who had been shopping or doing business in Tripoli. For them, it is now no more than a rather expensive bus-service.

What straightaway struck me when I first saw Ghadames was that it was so perfectly the real thing, a picture of an oasis remembered from my earliest school geography books: a mud-walled town crowded into a circumference of only four miles, thickly green with palm trees, water bubbling up and running everywhere – and outside the walls a reddish and golden-brown desert, flat, rock-strewn, completely barren, stretching away in all directions. In the distance are solitary hills, weathered flat and stranded like whales. At the tiny air-strip the plane was met by the airport manager, a Frenchman dressed in bright blue cloak and Tuareg habit, who affects a monkish or medieval style of haircut, and who because of this rig I at first took to be the Catholic Bishop of Ghadames (though, as one might imagine, no such person exists). The one hotel is within walking distance, but guests are put in a Land-Rover and driven along the half-mile of dusty track to get there.

Despite the airport and the hotel, Ghadames now is much as it must have been two or three hundred years ago – with the addition of a few trucks, a few policemen housed in the ex-Italian fort outside the walls, and a Spanish doctor who has a bungalow in the same part of 'New Ghadames'. Cydamae, the Roman posting-station, had a fort, which may or may not be the ruined tower on the north-east side of Ghadames: cylindrical and built in steps, it has an open platform at the top, a tiled floor covered with what looks like Roman cement, and a water-container set in the floor. At ground level there is a tunnel entrance, but it seemed blocked and I had no torch to find out. All round the flat gravelly plain beyond the walls, I found evidence of yet earlier settlement: beautifully worked Neolithic flints, leaf-shaped and finely flaked.

The town itself as it now stands was the creation of the Tuareg, the nomadic desert people who range over the inland areas of Algeria, Tunisia and Tripolitania. One story goes that some Tuareg were on their way across the desert after they had settled for the night and had their evening meal on the site of Ghadames. Next morning, when they were a few miles on their journey again, they realized that they had left some of their cooking-pots behind by mistake, so one of the group went back on his camel to recover them. As he was picking up the pots, his camel pawed the ground, and the traveller noticed to his amazement that where the camel scuffed the sand water bubbled up out of the ground. The whole area was a mass of artesian springs. And popular etymology says that Ghadames means 'the place where we ate last night'. The original spring is called Ain el Fras, 'the spring of the mare'.

But the Tuareg didn't live in the town: they were always tent-dwellers, and still are. They put their slaves and followers into the tall stone and mud tenements they built, and remained outside as shepherds and hunters, while their slaves from the Fezzan and the Sudan and the coastal belt cultivated the fertile gardens inside the walls. The present inhabitants of Ghadames – there are about 3,500 of them – are of mixed blood and are in part descendants of the slaves; but the Tuareg come only to shop and talk and stride through the narrow alleys, looking too tall and loose-limbed for such a constricted place. They wear long blue and white robes and their faces are swathed in black, so that only their eyes can be seen: a sinister touch. The women, on the other hand, are unveiled.

Inside the town, the upper levels of the houses and the roofs are for the women, who are seldom seen at ground level except when they go with buckets and jugs to collect water from the springs, or when they wash clothes in the little stone-cut cubicles which lie at the sides of the alleyways. Down below the flat roof-tops it's all tunnels and semi-darkness, and here the men sit and snooze out of the sun. The place is a labyrinth, a warren. Every so often you come out into a patch of open ground where the walls of the houses abut in such a way that a narrow shaft goes up to the sunlight. But the sun isn't welcome: where some of the covered alleys broaden out for a moment into little open squares, there are small vaulted piazzas with stone seats cut into the walls, alcoves deliberately trapping the shade.

It is easy to get lost, walking down these dark covered alleys. You walk for about twenty yards, and then perhaps attracted by some decorative detail on the white plaster arches you branch off down a passageway, which comes to a dead end at a high blank wall, or you are suddenly confronted by a handsome massive door and no way out but to turn round and go back the way you came. Strangers are so unusual in Ghadames that several times I was disconcerted by children screaming and scuttling down side-alleys at the sight of me.

Nevertheless, there is the one hotel, the 'Ain el Fras', which was built by the Italians in the nineteen-thirties: it was Italian publicists who called Ghadames 'the Pearl of the Desert'. It is small, dark inside, incorporating traditional Ghadames features, such as the tiny deeply-cut triangular windows and the horned white finials on the roofs; and it has reasonable food and a bar, beyond which is a room with a few showcases of local interest – flints, old flintlock rifles as used by the Tuareg, 'roses of the desert' (calcified fossils of coral-like plants), some local pottery, and examples of the massive keys and locks used on Ghadames doors. Everywhere, here and elsewhere in Ghadames, one sees palm-tree logs used, as roof-beams, lintels, and doors; some of the doors are embossed with big decorative nail-heads, scratched and chased. And there is a repeated range of white plaster decorative motifs, used in the walls and arches, done with moulds: the hand of Fatima, the star of David, feet, fish, and many abstract shapes – lattice-work of triangles and circles, lozenges, some formalized branch and leaf patterns. Old columns are incorporated into lintels, bench-ends, angle-corners, or in some cases the capitals (often Roman or Byzantine, seemingly) are simply left lying about in the town squares.

In the few Ghadames shops, most of the 'local craft' things come from over the border, from Algeria and Tunisia, only a few miles away; for Ghadames lies in the extreme tip of a small salient thrusting between its two neighbours. Here one can find pottery, Tuareg knives and swords, bright striped rugs and blankets. No pottery is made in Ghadames today, but some schoolboys told me that the last potter died only recently, and in a shop which announced on a battered board outside SOLDING OLD THINGS I bought a jug glazed yellow and green, exactly like one in the ethnographic section of the Castello Museum in Tripoli: it had been made in Ghadames, but it was anyone's guess when – perhaps some time in the nineteenth century.

If you keep on northwards down the tunnelled alleys you emerge among the garden-plots and palm trees, where water is conducted along open aqueducts standing waist high. Apparently there was some talk after the war about piping the water underground, but the inhabitants didn't take to the idea: they like to see their water quite clearly bubbling on its way – I suppose it reinforces the whole miracle of water in the desert. Beyond the vegetable gardens and palm groves are the abandoned plots, abandoned not because of lack of water but because there's no one to work them: the population of Ghadames is shrinking as the young people go off to find work in Tripoli or among the oil companies farther south, round Serdeles for example. And beyond the abandoned gardens are the crumbling houses and mud walls of an older Ghadames, and beyond them the rubbish dumps, now great cones of sand, where I scrabbled out pieces of glazed medieval Islamic pottery, reminiscent of the dusty heaps of sherds outside Cairo at Fustat. Finally, before the desert begins its bare, uncluttered, inhuman sweep across the landscape, there are the cemeteries, old and new, a few of them marked by a white domed *marabout* or holy man's tomb, but mostly simply acres of small standing stones, not even cairns or mounds, uninscribed, anonymous, gradually swallowed up by the drifting sand.

Coming back to Tripoli by air, flying at about 2,000 feet, I saw gazelles, the ruins of abandoned Berber villages, and the harsh plateau of the Hamada el Hamra – 'the red desert' – suddenly collapsing into the sharply indented escarpment of the Jebel Nefusa, split by its dozens of steeply descending wadis, most of which run themselves out in the plain: very few reach the sea, and none is a perennial stream. Far inland, perhaps a hundred miles north of Ghadames, I looked down and saw a solitary man, with no settlement, animal or vegetation anywhere in sight, walking across a waste of sand and rock. It seemed impossible that anyone or anything could survive down there in all that emptiness, but his tiny, sharply-focused figure seemed to be striding purposefully from somewhere to somewhere.

The Jebel Nefusa is an altogether bleaker and more savage mountain landscape than its Cyrenaican counterpart, the Jebel Akhdar. When the British army had garrisons in Tripolitania it was the favourite area for military exercises, and I spent three weeks there in the autumn of 1950, when my unit from Homs went under canvas about ten miles south of Garian. The road from Tripoli to Azizia, at the foot of the Jebel, is a dull and flat one, but then the sharp weathered crags rise over 2,000 feet out of the sea-level plain, almost sheer. The ascent is sharp and winding, curving spectacularly for about five miles until the final run into Garian village: a small, clean place, which used to be – and still is, to a lesser extent – a favourite summer retreat for rich families from Tripoli, who thus escape the humidity and intense heat of the plain.

But Garian and the area round about is chiefly known for its troglodyte settlements. Though one couldn't imagine it at a superficial glance, about half the population lives underground. As with the tomb-dwellers at Shahat in Cyrenaica, one perhaps tends to think of such living-conditions as being unremittingly primitive, and that they must necessarily go hand in hand with poverty. But this is not always so at Garian. The open-courtyard house centring on a well, with the rooms running off it, is typical of Libya: this is the plan followed at Garian, the only difference being that these 'houses' are forty feet or so deep in the ground, cut out of the rock and earth. Most of them are wired for electricity, and there are plans for piping water to them too: at present water has to be brought from wells at a distance, but this situation is no different from that found in many parts of Libya. The advantages of a shaft-house are real enough. In less peaceful times they could easily be defended against attack, since the tunnels leading down to them are narrow, and they are cool in summer and can be kept warm in winter – the winds in winter are keen in the Jebel Nefusa, there is sometimes frost, and snow isn't unknown. And more rooms can be added simply by tunnelling into the side of one's house.

I never penetrated a lived-in troglodytic dwelling, but it is very rare anyway for an urban Libyan to invite one into his home, whether below ground or above it: cafés are the places for social meeting, and the house is the preserve of the family and its own affairs. But once, when I climbed down the ramp into an abandoned one, I suffered from the assaults of an enemy commonly found in abandoned houses, caves and tombs: enormous red camel-fleas, each of which apparently bit me once and then vanished. I've no reason to suppose that they are such a menace to those who actually live below ground, and in any case the flea is everywhere a fairly common Libyan hazard, though never, I found, to quite the extent that Gwyn Williams did in his *Green Mountain*: Williams seems to have been more than normally flea-prone.

To the east, the Jebel comes closer to the sea: at Garian it is about sixty miles away, but towards Homs it comes much nearer, with lower and more broken foothills, and here, near the Wadi Gsea, is one of the inland areas which the Italians attempted to farm as intensively as they did the Tripolitanian coast. Marconi is the centre of one such area, and near it are many ruins of Roman farmhouses which show that continuity of development which was dear to the hearts of the pre-war Italian propagandists. I spent a couple of short leaves from the army – which seemed so bewildered by my activities that it never stood in my way – helping on a dig here, run by Olwen Brogan and David Oates. What they were doing can be seen in detail in the appropriate numbers of the British School at Rome's *Papers*,* but from my point of view it was my introduction to properly organized excavation outside England, where everything is laid on and you tend to have a solid phalanx of sightseers peering down at every shovelful you bring up.

The journey from Homs south-west to Marconi takes about an hour and a half for the forty miles, through hilly scrub country, with small settlements of mud huts and tents; the road is rough, slow and dusty. But once one comes into the valley of Marconi, the whole scene changes: the road becomes firm and well-laid,

* e.g. Vol. XXII: New Series Vol. IX, 1954.

the olive trees are ranged in orderly rows, each with its little scooped irrigation pit, and grapevines sprawl in their long furrows. The neat white buildings appear, the farmhouse bungalows of the former colonists, each with the initials I.N.F.P.S. (Industria Nazionale Fascista Providenzia Sala) and fasces in white plaster on the right of the door, and its number on the left. At that time, in 1950, each house also bore the Roman numeral XVII, to commemorate its being built in 1939, the seventeenth year of Fascist rule; but these have been largely hacked away or defaced, though Tripolitania has been less zealous about removing such traces than has Cyrenaica. The village-centre itself is of the basic Italian/Tripolitanian pattern: a square bordered on two sides by a police station, a general store, a small clinic, a simple church, and the *albergo*, where the party of British archaeologists slept and ate.

It would be dishonest if I didn't point out here that all my contacts with the ex-colonial families, both at Marconi and at Crispi (near Misurata), were pleasant and friendly, and that at this period the relationship between at least the Tripolitanian Italians and the Libyans always seemed trusting and even warm. The Cyrenaican settlers had been evacuated during the war, never to return; but in Tripolitania the atmosphere had been such that it was possible for the Italians to go on farming.

Of the four labourers used by Olwen Brogan and David Oates, three were Arab and one was Italian: Mohammed, Mlud, Feraj, and Battista. They worked together well, and spoke that *lingua franca* of Italian laced with Arabic (or vice versa) which we also soon adopted. The site chosen was seven miles up the Wadi Gsea south of Marconi, on a hillside where there stood four massive walls among a heap of rubble, two orthostats of an olive-press still standing, and a number of others collapsed, a couple of water cisterns, a rock-cut well, and many outbuildings, in varying stages of decay. The work was heavy because of the amount of rock. One of the inscriptions we uncovered is now in the Castello Museum in Tripoli: apparently an early Christian tombstone, it carries the abbreviated words DOMINBENIF, and the outline of a carved hand, much like the hand of Fatima, the Prophet's daughter, which is so common a symbol throughout Islamic Libya. It is certainly pre-Islamic and even pre-Roman, when it is sometimes taken to be a symbol of Tanit, the Phoenician goddess.

One brilliant July morning I saw, on the opposite hillside, a small shepherd boy with his sheep and goats, walking slowly along playing his pipes – the *magruna* – and the weird wailing drone through the clear air suddenly seemed to lift me into another existence, pastoral and remote. I have heard the *magruna* many times since, coming from wedding feasts and picnic parties, on student expeditions and on 'folklorist' radio programmes, but it has never had quite the force of that first experience as I lay back in the dry, pungent smell of the scrub and saw that boy by the Wadi Gsea. Mukhtar, the mess-servant at Kassala, brought me a pair when I told him that I was looking for pipes, but they were stolen just before my demob. ship sailed – presumably by some homeward-bound souvenir-hunter. And when, fifteen years later, I bought a pair in the Tripoli *souk*, it seemed only a gesture towards my past. The things had lost their magic.

It was in the square at Marconi that I saw the arrival by ambulance (or rather, a Land-Rover roughly converted into one) of an extremely ill old man who had been brought in from one of the outlying tents up the Wadi Gsea. It turned out that he had had a large meal of *kous-kous*, the natural accompaniment to which is copious quantities of water, and had then complained of severe abdominal pains. The doctor at the Marconi clinic, an Italian, decided to operate, which seemed drastic, but it was the right action. When the old man was opened up they drained over twenty pints of fluid out of him: the water had been swelling unbearably the semolina of the *kous-kous*, and once it was released the pressure and the pain disappeared. After a few hours rest, the man was whisked back to his tent in the Land-Rover, lucky to be alive, so the doctor said.

Back on the coast, the road from Homs to the Cyrenaican provincial border at Marble Arch is over 350 miles, at first through the settled country of the *Ente Colonizazzione Libya* with its bungalows, ploughed fields, and orchards. Round Zliten and Misurata there are thick palm groves, and shortly before Zliten the wide mouth of the Wadi Caam, with its ruined Roman waterworks and barrage. This was the source of one of the aqueducts to Leptis, twelve miles away, and also the place where the Greeks made their earliest attempt to settle in Tripolitania, which was otherwise a Phoenician and Carthaginian area. Herodotus tells how in 520 B.C. Dorieus, the son of the Spartan king Anaxandridas, having quarrelled with his brother who had succeeded to the throne, decided to leave Sparta, taking with him a number of his countrymen. Guided by Greek islanders from Thera (which was also the source of the Greek colonies in Cyrenaica under Battus), Dorieus disembarked in Tripolitania at the mouth of the Wadi Caam, or *Cinyps* as Herodotus calls it, where he founded a colony. But the colony lasted only three years, for the Carthaginians joined with the native Libyan tribe of Macae, and drove the colonists into the sea.

There is no archaeological evidence for this story, and D. E. L. Haynes* throws doubt on it: why is there no mention of Leptis, only twelve miles away, having taken part in the colony's destruction, and why was Carthage's reaction so slow? At any rate, there is no trace anywhere in Tripolitania of the Greeks ever having got even a foothold, and the present border between Tripolitania and Cyrenaica is traditionally that fixed by agreement between the Cyreneans and the Carthaginians some time towards the end of the fifth century B.C. 'Marble Arch', the extraordinary oriental gateway built by Mussolini to mark the border on the coast road, is near the two 'Tombs of the Philainoi': two mounds which were popularly supposed to mark the graves of the Carthaginian brothers who died as a result of a strange – and probably legendary – boundary settlement. The story (again from Herodotus) is that after much pointless fighting Cyrene and Carthage decided to settle the matter by simultaneously dispatching runners, who would fix the frontier at the point where they met. Somehow the Philainoi managed to make much better speed than their Cyrenean rivals, and had covered two-thirds greater a distance when they met. The Cyreneans accused the Carthaginians of having cheated, at which the Carthaginians asked for a further test, to be agreeable to both sides; and the Greek proposal was that the Philainoi should either submit to burial alive at the point where the Carthaginians wished to draw the frontier, or that they should allow the Greeks to advance as far as they wanted on the same conditions. The Philainoi accepted the challenge, and where

* *Ancient Tripolitania*, pp. 24–5

✳ 96

they were buried two altars were raised to them. The frontier has been along the line of their burial ever since.

A good Herodotean tale, whatever the truth of it. At the border today there is still the atmosphere of a frontier-post, despite the fact that Tripolitania and Cyrenaica are merely provinces of one kingdom. But that 'merely' gives the wrong impression, for the passport-checking and registration at Marble Arch is a real part of the ancient conflict and suspicion between the areas, separated from the beginning by the wide barren block of the Sirtica, where the desert and the sea join.

On the Tripolitanian side, the tussocky, sandy area begins soon after Misurata; to the east of the road are low, brackish lagoons, and a track here follows the five miles to Tauorga, a mud-walled oasis without streets or public buildings, simply squat mud huts roofed with palm branches and matting. Here the mats and baskets sold in Misurata are woven, from the rushes that encircle the village. The atmosphere is more like that of some equatorial African *kraal* than an Arab village, and the feeling of isolation is far greater than the distance from Misurata and the highway might make one suppose. Beyond the turning to Tauorga you begin the long slog east across a landscape so featureless that after a stop for the night or for a meal you have to think twice about which direction you are going: there are no landmarks to guide you, just the man-made strip of tarmac with its white kilometre posts, and many of these have been so weathered or defaced that they are no longer legible. At Bu Grein – nothing but filling stations and a few shacks – the Fezzan road begins, going down past the biggest Roman fort in Tripolitania, Bu Ngem, and on to Sebha. After Bu Grein, Buerat, whose Italian military ruins look from a distance like a large town, but when you come near you see that it's nothing but a shell, with the dunes drifting close. Sand is such a problem along the Sirtica stretch of the road that here and there the dunes have been stabilized by planting a chess-board pattern of tenacious grasses, a slow method, and one which the oil-companies are trying to replace with that of spraying with oil, which quickly gives a firm surface but is, of course, more expensive. But in a country as quickly rich as Libya, speed is often preferable to cheapness.

In another fifty miles Sirte is reached: a Roman outpost, though nothing remains of it above ground except for a few carved capitals left lying about in the public squares. Yet Sirte has a firmer identity as a town than anywhere else between Misurata and Agedabia, and it even has a small hotel – but a filthy and neglected one. On one journey through we stopped for a drink and to do some shopping in the *souk*, when we were approached by a confident-looking man who said: 'You Englishman? You from London? Preston, Birmingham, London', then stopped abruptly and walked briskly away. The small square of shops which is the centre of Sirte is fresh, white and clean, with purple bougainvillea festooned over the shop-fronts, flocks of terracotta sheep wandering about, and crowds of children who like nothing better than following an itinerant foreigner to see what he's going to do next; though rebuked by their elders for rudeness, they have trailed after me, sometimes giggling but usually just staring out of their huge hollow eyes, occasionally wiping away with a sleeve the long rope of snot descending from nose to mouth. It's very rare to be pursued with shouts or whines of *'bakshish'*, and indeed Leptis, Tolmeita and Apollonia are the only places in the whole of Libya where I remember such importunings: a strong contrast with Egypt and other Middle Eastern countries.

The site of Medina Sultan, a settlement which was in turn Punic, Roman, and early Islamic, lies off the road towards the sea thirty-five miles east of Sirte. All that remains today are two Islamic forts and a wide scatter of stones and sherds. This was the place which the eleventh-century Arab historian El-Bekri described as:

A large city situated beside the sea, and enclosed by a wall
of bricks, containing a mosque, a bath and several bazaars.
It has three gates, of which one faces the south, another the
north, and the third – a small one – leads to the sea. This
city has no suburbs but possesses date-palms, gardens, sweet-
water springs, and a large number of cisterns.

But a century later Edrisi described it as 'in a miserable condition and containing only a few inhabitants', and by the first half of the thirteenth century another Arab historian wrote that it 'is one of the ancient cities mentioned in books. The Arabs have destroyed it, and there remain only some castles in which the Arabs have established their residence'. This record of gradual decay seems to point to the effect of the invasion of the Beni Hilal and Beni Suleim, those tribes who came out of Arabia in the eleventh century, passed into Upper Egypt, and then were encouraged by the Fatimid Caliphate to reconquer Tripolitania and Tunisia from the Berbers, who had managed to assert their independence against the descendants of the original seventh-century Arab invaders under Amr Ibn el-As. The Beni Hilal moved into the western regions, while the Beni Suleim mostly stayed in Cyrenaica, the migration being – as Arab historians put it – 'like locusts or wolves'. Their coming meant the end of settled life in Libya for many centuries: the nomad had come with his goats and his tents, and to him all buildings were foreign. It is from these two tribes that the modern Libyan can derive himself.

When I saw Medina Sultan, there were rather depressing traces of Antiquities Department activities on the site: cement reconstructions in process of being built, and an entirely unsuitable brick wall. But I was pleased to see a Bedouin come up on his donkey to fill his water-canisters at the ancient well which stood in the middle of the reconstructed main square, oblivious, I'm sure, of the part his ancestors must have played in reducing the town to the unimpressive waste it is today. To him, no doubt, as to most *Muslimin* in Libya, all such ruins are taken to be older than Islam and therefore *Kuffara* – heathen. No one but a heathen bothers about heathen ruins, and this is the constant battle the Libyan Department of Antiquities has to fight, against the depredations of farmers, builders, road-contractors, and even other government departments. Yet the Bedouin at the well unconsciously made a sort of continuity in a way that the renovatory efforts of the archaeologists did not.

The road east of the turning to Medina Sultan temptingly indicates NAWFALIYAH on kilometre stone after kilometre stone, as if announcing some grand emporium of the desert, some desirable oasis after the mile upon mile of wind-patterned sand-hills and flat rock; but then a signpost to the right indicates that Nawfaliyah is not on the highway at all, but somewhere to the south out of sight. Frustrated on one journey by this unseen place, the name of which had become imprinted on our minds through the repetition of those white stones, we swung off down

✳ 99

the narrow turning, and after seven miles reached a ruined Italian fort, a few low stone huts, a windpump, and a flat, open stretch round it where dozens of camels, donkeys, and goats congregated. This was Nawfaliyah. A few men were desultorily clearing sand from the road, which came to an end in shallow dunes. The whole purpose of the place was water, for the flocks and herds brought there, and to be loaded into the donkeys' metal canisters, oil-drums, jerry-cans, skins and bottles and tall jugs. Evidently the road had been built by the Italians to serve their now shattered garrison, but the wells had existed before them and looked like continuing long after them. This was the irreducible Libya: scrawny animals at a watering place, in a featureless landscape where the only wealth was in beasts and the only impulse mobility.

Yet not far away, at Ras Lanuf, the big silver tankers lie offshore and absorb the new wealth of oil from the deep desert wells. Tarmac airstrips run by the road, a U.S. Coastguard station flies the Stars and Stripes, and the tall horned arch at the Cyrenaican border indicates a more complex world. This is the littered edge of things, with skeletons of animals and of cars lying abandoned by the roadside, fallen telegraph poles, and the civilized scurf of whisky and beer bottles jettisoned to left and right. A Muslim may drink, by civil if not by religious law, in Tripolitania; but not in Cyrenaica, older and stricter in its observances.

On through Agheila – where Keith Douglas describes the infantry reporting 'some Christmas presents, pleasant and unpleasant' (booty and booby-traps) – across a flat plain to Beshr, Brega – where the cross-roads lead north to the Esso oil-port of Marsa Brega and south to the oilfields at Zelten – and Agedabia. Here it is dull, undulating, tussocky country, enlivened sometimes by a couple of gazelles bounding across the road and swiftly merging into the landscape, or by a grey big-brushed desert fox. But Agedabia itself, for all its ancient importance as a Roman station, a post on the caravan route, and the capital of the puppet Cyrenaican régime the Italians attempted to create in 1920, is a miserable town. There is a ruined fortress-palace of Fatimid date close by, but what I chiefly remember of it is a wretchedly cold night in January spent just on the edge of the town, when the driver of the Taunus microbus 'taxi' in which I was travelling from Tripoli to Benghazi suddenly decided at about midnight that he had had enough for one day and wouldn't travel on to Benghazi until tomorrow. My travelling companions, all of whom were farmers going back to the Jebel Akhdar, got out, wrapped themselves like cocoons in their white *jallabiyah*, lay down on the bare ground and immediately went to sleep; while I – encouraged as a favour to bed down on the front seat of the vehicle – shivered so violently that the whole machine rocked. Agedabia next morning, though under a blue sky, looked bleak, depressed and run-down. I have seen it in happier circumstances, but it has never seemed much improved.

The last hundred miles to Benghazi, through Magrun, Ghemines and Tika, is dullish, but a turning at Ghemines leads to Solluch, fifteen miles away: an odd place, almost entirely an Italian creation, and the terminus of the south-eastern branch railway which they built from Benghazi. Now the tracks abruptly come to an end by hanging over an embankment, though the station looks ready to receive passengers or goods at any moment – for some reason it was being painted on my most recent visit there, though the last train ran long ago. It was just outside Solluch, on the bare plain now covered with flocks and herds, that Omar Mukhtar, the great patriot-leader of the Cyrenaicans in their guerrilla warfare against the Italians, was executed on September 16th, 1931. He was an old man in his late sixties when he was finally caught in the high Jebel near Gasr esc-Sciahden; he was wounded, pinned down by his fallen horse, captured, and taken to Solluch. There, still suffering from his wounds, he was hanged in the presence of 20,000 Bedouin and Cyrenaican leaders, who had been specially brought up from the concentration camps at Brega and Agheila to witness the *coup de grâce* being given to their resistance. It was the end of twenty years of almost continuous war, and it effectively ended the period of 'pacification'. After the Second World War Omar Mukhtar's remains were brought from Solluch and were buried inside the huge pink carbuncle of a tomb that lies at the end of Sharia Amr Ibn el-As in Benghazi. On the very spot where he was hanged at Solluch stands a small white column on which a commemorative tablet is set: these are strangely neglected and even defaced, though by visitors who want to show that they have visited the place rather than by wanton political action. Libya is indeed a palimpsest of *graffiti*: back on the main road, just past Ghemines, a monitory notice can still be seen painted on the side of a crumbling pink-washed building:

> You will not laff
> If Jerry straffs
> Safety first
> Stay dispersed.

Seeing it, one drives the last few miles into Benghazi in chastened mood.

6   Tribes and Loyalties

A CLASSROOM in a Tripoli secondary school. The school-master, a blunt straightforward Yorkshireman, is preparing the boys for the *Taujihia*, the Libyan school-leaving certificate, and the textbook is a simplified version of Lamb's *Tales from Shakespeare*. They are just about to start *Hamlet*, and Metcalf is trying to give them some idea about the motivation of the play. 'Now, supposing you were married, and very much loved your wife, and you thought your wife loved you, and then you suddenly died: what would you expect your wife to do?' A coal-black boy from the Fezzan in the front row at once raises his hand: 'Sir, she should wait one month, and then she should marry my brother.'

One starts with mutual incomprehension, and with a greater or lesser degree of goodwill. The Libyan, particularly the Cyrenaican (who is still a Bedouin at heart if not in fact), is not a volatile man or one who wears his heart on his sleeve. He is attached to his family, his tribe, his region, his religion: nowhere in Islam can greater devoutness, and greater conservatism of faith, be found. Patriotism – the concept of 'being a Libyan' – is another matter. The forced unification by the Italians and the political unification after independence in 1951 haven't yet satisfactorily welded together a state with common identifications and common aims. What has been shared in the past has been oppression and neglect, for five hundred years of Turkish rule and thirty of Italian.

The traveller who arrives by air at Benina on his way to Benghazi can see almost as soon as he leaves the airport a reminder of what Libya has had to survive to reach its present condition. As you turn through Benina village into the long straight run of fourteen miles towards Benghazi, mirage-like in the distance, above the walls of the Italian fort on the right the top of a heavy wooden gallows can be glimpsed. Here, in the second Italo-Senussi war of 1923–32, the daily quota of 'rebels' was hanged. I never discovered whether the gallows had been left up out of simple inertia or as a memorial to the insulted patriot dead. Like many things in Libya, both explanations may well be true.

Other people see the patriots differently. My wife was sent a copy of *House and Garden* with a feature about the Tripoli villa of the Contessa Anna Maria Cicogna Volpi, the daughter of the man who was for five years Governor of Tripolitania and who effectively crushed Tripolitanian resistance so that only Omar Mukhtar and his Cyrenaican guerrillas ('the army of the night', as they were known) were left to carry on the struggle. There, in the Villa Volpi, among the trappings of that odd nineteen-twentyish Italo-Arab architecture, with its imported Genoese tiles and its tasteful bits of Libyan 'folk culture', the Contessa apparently bewitched her interviewer into swallowing the Volpi version of history, for Mr Roderick Cameron writes:

> Conte Giuseppe Volpi was responsible for unifying the people who, under the Turks, had split up into warring factions that terrorized the countryside. In 1922 Volpi succeeded in trapping the guerrilla bands and forcing them into battle. The encounter took place at Misurata, a coastal village from which Volpi took the title Conte di Misurata . . .

'Unifying the people' is one way of putting it: one might with greater accuracy describe Volpi's activities with another of Mr Cameron's terms – 'terrorizing'. That his daughter could return to the Villa Volpi after the war ('My first sight of it in 1948 was almost too much for me . . . It had been occupied by troops, and you can imagine what a wreck I was faced with'), and still continues to spend part of each year there, shows how effective the pacification was. Those dissidents who had not been killed in battle, hanged, or put in the barbed-wire pens of the Brega and El Agheila concentration camps in Cyrenaica, had largely fled to Egypt and other parts of the Arab world. Those who were left either actively collaborated or, more commonly, just went on living as best they could with no more contact with the Italians than they could help.

Fifteen years ago, at the time of independence, Libya was a society of peasants and small shopkeepers on the coast and Bedouins elsewhere. For more than five hundred years Libyans had had no voice in political affairs, except for the brief period in the eighteenth century when the Karamanli family established a sort of oligarchy – and then only within Tripoli and its immediate environs. Though some tribes considered themselves to carry more weight than others, the general condition of poverty and subservience achieved a casteless and classless levelling unique in the Arab world, and the results of this remain today; for though Libya can't, in any accurate political sense, be considered a true parliamentary democracy, the attitude and behaviour of Libyans to one another is truly democratic. They have no notion of one man being 'better' than another because of birth or position, for in the lifetime of anyone over twenty-five all have been a subject people. Wealth is respected, and to a certain extent age, but equal with these is the respect paid to a man who follows *arkan*, the five pillars of Islam, particularly fasting in the month of Ramadan and, most conspicuously, *Haj* – the pilgrimage to Mecca. The crossing-sweeper or the *ghaffir* may be a crossing-sweeper or a *ghaffir*, but if he has been to the sanctuary at Mecca he is also a *Haj*, and is addressed as such: 'the venerable', as it were, rather than plain *essayid*, or Mr.

Haj, incidentally, is one of the most conspicuous signs of Islam in Libya. Pilgrims are subsidized, on the basis of a sort of means test, and special ships are hired by the Libyan government to pick them up at Tripoli and Benghazi for the voyage to Jedda, the port for Mecca. At the time of *Haj*, the streets of Benghazi are full of cars and vans flying white pennants to show they are going on pilgrimage; and the families from which pilgrims have gone put up white flags for the whole period their folk are away. They flutter equally above smart villa in Fueihat, shack in Berka, and Bedouin tent. Pilgrimage exacts the same tribute from all.

The other great Islamic leveller in Libya is Ramadan, the twenty-nine days of fasting which, in the Muslim calendar, shift with the year, so that it may fall in the winter (as it did in 1965 and 1966) or in the summer, with all the privations that that brings with it. Generally it is very strictly observed, following the Koranic injunction: 'Eat and drink until so much of the dawn appears that a white thread may be distinguished from a black. Then keep the fast completely until night.' The pattern of Ramadan is exhausting, disrupting life completely. My students would eat, drink and smoke almost the whole night, and then either turn up to classes late, wan and half-asleep, or not at all. Government working-hours are cut, many shops are closed until dusk. Yet it was very rare for me to come across any complaints about the observation of the fast: several students said that it made them feel better, more alive, though this was often belied by their appearance, which was not so much the result of austerity as of lack of sleep and indigestion. Yet, however it was interpreted, it united the nation, from the Rector to Saad, our one-eyed and impoverished *ghaffir*.

Within a single *'aila* or sub-clan, a whole range of people with widely different jobs and incomes can be found, but their lineage, which is what unites them, outweighs whatever divisions of status and money there might appear to be. For example, the Rector of the University (who towards the end of my time was appointed Minister of Education) had one relative who was a *feraj* (a servant, responsible for cleaning, bringing tea, and so on) in the University library, and another, Hawa, a woman who came twice a week to do our washing. Mustafa Baiou, the Rector, had been educated at universities in Egypt and America: Hawa was illiterate. But both traced their origins to the same *'aila* in Misurata (from which Benghazi was settled in the fifteenth century), and though this seemed to make no practical difference to Hawa's existence – for she was desperately poor, in circumstances I shall deal with in a moment – she 'belonged' to her *'aila* and that fact was the important thing in her life.

Most of the political and much of the social life of the country is based on tribal groupings and loyalties. In the second chamber, or House of Representatives, of the *Majlis*, most of the fifty-five members – especially those from Cyrenaica – are in effect elected by the bigger tribes, which select their candidates after consultation among the sheikhs. There are no political parties, only tribal lobbies. So it is possible for a man in an insignificant position but with high standing and respect in his tribe to reach the legislature. An example of this was told me not long after my arrival in Benghazi, by an English expatriate who retailed the story as an example of the absurd goings-on one is likely to come across in Libya, though to me it seemed much more an illustration of the fact that the country, though in some ways an oligarchic dictatorship, in others is more sensibly in the hands of the people than many that call themselves democratic.

It seemed that Watson and his wife employed a houseboy – an unlikeable term, especially when applied to a man in his early forties, as Ali was. When the Watsons went back to England for a long spell of leave, they paid Ali off and said goodbye, hoping that he might work for them again when they returned to Benghazi, though of course it was impossible to make a firm arrangement for a time six months away. Back in Benghazi again after their leave, there was no sign of Ali, until one day Watson was driving through Berka, the south-eastern suburb of the town, when he saw the familiar figure stepping out of the back of a chauffeur-driven Mercedes. Stopping and greeting him, Watson noticed that he was smartly dressed in what looked like a good Savile Row suit. Ali seemed delighted to see his old employer, and they stood chatting on the pavement until Watson rather wistfully said it looked unlikely that he would be coming back to be their houseboy. 'Ah yes, I am afraid so, sir,' Ali replied. 'You see, I am now a member of the House of Representatives, and I must spend much time in Beida.'

The power and influence of the tribe and family reach into most corners of Libyan life. The person who 'slips down the crack' (as a friend put it) between tribe and tribe or family and family, through alienation or ostracism, is lost. Hawa was such a case. Her brother had quarrelled with her husband, and in a fit of anger had killed him. Therefore a state of feud existed between the two families, and neither would have anything to do with Hawa. There are still relics of blood-feud, even in urban areas. Though there is a longer tradition of town or village settlement along the Tripolitanian coastal strip, which works against the continuance of tribal traditions, in Cyrenaica the great majority of the inhabitants of Benghazi are first- or second-generation nomads, and they carry with them into the huts and alleys of the town ways of life long established in the Jebel and the desert.

Our friend Ramadan Zubi came round one night and told us about the grim incident which broke up a Benghazi wedding where he, as a family member, was a guest a few days earlier. Another of the guests – and not a member of the family – was a lieutenant in the immigration police, a man who because of his position was allowed to carry a revolver, and whose speciality at weddings was to fire this off in the air as a sign of excitement and celebration. This particular wedding was being held at a house in one of the narrow streets round the corner from our block, with overhanging balconies. The immigration lieutenant had been warned by one of the family (himself a colonel in the civil police) not to indulge in his usual habit because of the narrowness of the street and the crowded balconies overhead. The twelve-year-old nephew of the bridegroom got out on to one of these balconies to watch the scene below better, and was standing there when the lieutenant, in the heat of the moment, forgot all prudence and whipped out his revolver, firing it into the air. The bullet went straight through the boy's head, but did not kill him instantly. The lieutenant, realizing what he had done, and fearing that the family would assault him, immediately fled to the officers' club in Sharia Omar Mukhtar, where he made a complete statement and handed himself over.

There followed a hectic race to save the boy's life. Ramadan said that the Italian doctor who perfunctorily looked at the boy at the municipal hospital gave as his only reaction the statement that in any case the boy's brain was so damaged that even if he lived he would be completely paralysed. So nothing was done in Benghazi. The sole hope was to fly the boy to brain surgery in Rome or London, so Ramadan and other members of the family managed to get in touch with the Italian consul – who had to be woken up in the middle of the night – and within a few hours secured a visa and a flight to Rome. But by the time they returned the boy was dead.

The rest was in doubt. The lieutenant was held in Benghazi Prison, would go on trial, and would almost certainly be sentenced. But if the boy's family was dissatisfied with the court's sentence, Ramadan said, they would meet to decide on a fit punishment of their own when the man was released. In other words, he might have to answer with his own life, and the family conference would decide who was to kill him. Or it might be that another member of the lieutenant's family would be picked as the victim, even before the prisoner was released from jail. Though Ramadan was quick to say that he himself didn't approve of such a blood-feud, he said that both families were Bedouin, and that though the Benghazi branch of the boy's tribe was an urbanized and even 'liberal' one (the boy's mother, for example, being the headmistress of the primary school at Benina), the main part of the tribe centred on the plain round Barce and was traditional in its observances.

Even when there is not a blood-feud, there can be blood money. The brother of one of my students accidentally knocked over and killed a boy with his car. The student's family was compelled by the boy's family to hand over £1,600, quite apart from the punishment exacted by the civil court. And the German employee of the local engineering firm was put in the same position when he ran over another boy near Barce. He spent some time in Benghazi Prison, though luckily he had his firm solidly on his side and they paid both the civil fine and the compensation to the family.

Although such private codes of punishment (and their tacit acceptance by the authorities) will no doubt die out in time, they and the tribal attitudes that go with them are still tenacious. And 'the way of the tents', of the *bwadi* or Bedouin, is not necessarily marked by backwardness and ignorance, even when one imposes Western standards or gives a Western interpretation to what these words mean. A young English anthropologist came out from Durham University while we were living in Benghazi, to do field-work among the Bedouin. He was eventually given permission to live in a tented community south-east of Solluch, as long as he agreed to abide by the rule and customs of the family. Throughout the whole period of several months during which he lived in this way, he did not once so much as glimpse a woman, even in the distance: they were rigidly kept apart from the men, getting on with their cooking and spinning in the seclusion of their own tents, in an atmosphere very different from that in the tent I visited at Gasr Jeballa. In the sheikh's tent the young Englishman found a considerable library of books on theology and philosophy, on which the sheikh would learnedly and eloquently speak for hours on end. It turned out that this man, living deep in the unprofitable pre-desert among his camels and sheep, with only sporadic contact with towns and the ways of towns, was someone of not only deep but also wide knowledge, who had even published essays on Islamic history and faith. Such a man is of course a rarity among the Cyrenaican Bedouin, many of whom are illiterate (though their aural memory – of genealogy, of folk-poetry and folk-song, and of the Koran – is reputedly prodigious); but, after all, who was the Prophet Muhammed, in a sense, but a tribesman of the desert?

Still, the gradual move throughout Libya is to the towns, and

✳ 109

therefore to the food, manners, dress, and attitudes of the towns. One result of this too-rapid settlement by the poorer Bedouin is the great scummy ring of shanty housing round Benghazi and Tripoli; they have grown up quickly, and they go on growing, the clearest indication of the depopulation of the country and the growth of the towns in Libya; for whereas rural depopulation in England can be seen in abandoned farmhouses and derelict barns, in Libya the Bedouin country seems no more empty if two thousand leave it, or two hundred, or twenty. So, for example, Benghazi grew from a population of 23,000 in 1922 to 70,000 in 1962, and is at the time I am writing estimated at 150,000. Who these people are, and how they live, can be seen by going round El Kish or behind the side streets of Berka or round the ring road before the turning to Benina. They have exchanged their cool, water-resistant, airy tents for tottering structures made out of scraps of timber, jerry-cans, palm branches and fronds, sacking, and – if they can afford them – strips and sheets of zinc.

It was in a hut like this that Hawa lived in Berka, in a waste-land of such huts jammed end to end close by the big sweet factory owned by our landlord. In the strong winds and heavy rain one winter, her hut collapsed; and one day Pablo Foster and I went out to Berka to take her some zinc sheets with which to rebuild it. There were no roads, only narrow ginnels of mud running between the rows of huts, and here the children played, the yellow dogs snarled and snapped, women threw out rubbish, and men relieved themselves. The smell was appalling. Once the puddles and mud had dried, the whole place would be choked with dust. Incongruous hulks of abandoned cars were piled up along one 'street'. In the middle of all this was a single hand-pump, where every family had to raise its water. Hawa's hut had one foul mattress, slung across slats on the mud floor, and on it she and her three children slept: she had a married daughter elsewhere, and an older boy, who had got into trouble with the police several times and had been jailed, and whom Hawa had eventually thrown out. On the door of a hut near by, a medley of packing-cases and oil-drums, was painted the single word ALLAH: the heart of the faith even in this degradation. Professor Emrys Jones, writing about such shanty towns in Latin America* says: 'But

* *Towns and Cities*, Oxford, 1966.

however desperate the plight of their people, one point must be stressed. These are not slums in the conventional sense, but rather stages in city growth reflecting both the energy and the ability of the people.' It seems cold comfort at Berka.

Because these squatters' settlements inevitably lie on the edges of Benghazi and Tripoli, it's easy to ignore them in the centre, where the roads are swarming with Libyan-owned cars, from Mercedes – the sure symbol that a Libyan has arrived – to packs of small Fiats and Volkswagens. The Libyan, even the Bedouin Libyan (some of whom have found the inflationary price of sheep has made them rich men), has taken to the car as if it were a cherished animal, and he treats it with that mixture of pride and disregard which characterizes the common Arab attitude to working animals. To see a Libyan driver reversing his vehicle is to see a man mastering an uppish horse: up go the reins, down goes the whip, in go the heels, and with a scream of tyres and a snarl of gears the car shoots backwards at forty miles an hour. Then slam go the brakes, gears crash into first, and the shuddering, slavering beast is given its head.

Such old habits of attitude or action in new circumstances show themselves in other ways. In a rich Libyan family, living in a villa at Fueihat or Giorgimpopoli, there may be a television set (very expensive, and only feebly picking up Rome or Malta, or the canned comedies and patriotic exhortations of Wheelus Field A.F.N.); the furniture will be Italian imitations of Louis-the-someone; there will be crystal chandeliers, and perhaps three cars, and the head of the family may often be away on business in Cairo, Beirut, Athens, or London; but at a family meal, the food will be served from a common dish in the centre of the table, into which everyone dips his right hand to fetch out the meat. The desert is only a few years away, just around the corner in the past. And uniting all, whether in a silver frame in Fueihat or clipped from a magazine and pinned to the wall of a shanty store in El Kish, will be a picture of the King, the leader of a desert faith, and a desert brotherhood, the Senussiya.

The Senussi movement started in the second quarter of the nineteenth century, under the direction of the King's grandfather, who lived in Morocco and Algeria. Migrating to Cyrenaica specifically because it was empty and unspoiled country where

✳ III

meditation and asceticism might more properly be practised, the Grand Senussi found the area fertile for the faith, and soon *zawia*, or religious training-centres, were springing up throughout the province. There were a few in Tripolitania and the Fezzan, but on the whole it was the Cyrenaican Bedouin who embraced the new, stern teachings. In its origins, the Senussiya was not a political movement, but with the Italian invasion towards the end of 1911 it automatically became the rallying point for all devout Muslims, the ethical centre round which *jihad*, holy war, could be fought. When Libya eventually won its independence in 1951, with Idris as its acknowledged and acclaimed king, it was the force of the Senussi as much as anything that had achieved the new state.

The most holy shrine of the Senussiya is Jaghbub (often written in its Italianized form, Giarabub), 170 miles due south of Tobruk in the eastern part of Cyrenaica. At the behest of the King, the road has recently been made wider and well surfaced, though the only 'place' on the whole of the long drive south is El Adhem, the R.A.F. base and camp seventeen miles out of Tobruk, the last of the British military toeholds in Libya. This road runs through pebbly and gritty desert, at first with some patches of camelthorn, finally with no vegetation at all. Down it go the water-tankers from Tobruk, supplying fresh water to Jaghbub, which otherwise has only enough brackish water to support some inferior palm trees; and even this tanker water is not truly from Tobruk, but comes by raised pipeline along the 110 miles from Derna. The whole settlement of Jaghbub is – not necessarily in a pejorative sense – a parasitic one: almost everything except a small quantity of dates must come in from outside, and nothing is produced – except spirituality.

The shrine of the Grand Senussi, where the King's grand-father lies buried, can be seen from miles away as one drives south, its white cupola dazzlingly overtopping the oasis. The walls which surround it and the original Islamic university are also white-washed, and the whole of the 1856 foundation stands on a slight eminence within this wall, backed by higher flat-topped and weathered crags, tunnelled now with ammunition stores, filleted with foxholes, and littered with shells, cartridges, all the impervious paraphernalia of modern war. The Italians during the Second

World War desperately tried to hold Jaghbub, but were finally winkled out after repeated air assaults on these crags.

In the shrine, the exterior is stark, pure, the white wall of the entrance having something of the quality of a Mondrian painting, with the six windows, each with a simple curved orange lintel, spatially arranged in an asymmetrical yet satisfying balance. But the interior is almost garish, with elaborate glass and crystal chandeliers, the walls painted in bright colours in imitation of Islamic tiles, and the sepulchre itself seen through a glittering brass cage. The workmanship is Egyptian, not native, and is like a rather poverty-stricken imitation of the mosque of Mohamed Ali in Cairo. Yet beyond it, in a sort of ancillary chapel, the tombs of some of the Grand Senussi's followers seem like simple Bedouin tombs transplanted from the desert: roughly cut stones at head and foot, placed in the sand round which a low wall has been built. The contrast is extraordinarily moving: it is as if – to put it in another way – the shell of the shrine had been placed over the rude cairns of some desolate place, and the nomadic origins of the whole Senussi movement are suddenly seen isolated and heightened. Simplicity, isolation, high-minded poverty, the old-fashioned virtues of the Arab, romanticized by the English, and scarcely relevant to the urban world of the coastal strip, seem symbolized and fixed in the graves of Jaghbub. Only Tobruk has a stronger pull on one's graveyard emotions.

Tobruk is a strange place: to anyone who remembers the Second World War, the name itself has a resonance. And yet the town as it now stands, brash, modern and dusty, looped round a deeply indented natural harbour, holds nothing special. Its offices and port installations are almost entirely given over to oil companies: the Serir oilfield lies about three hundred miles south. Only in its outskirts, in what was the famous 'perimeter' of the wartime siege, does one begin to grasp something of its historical force: a rocky landscape, but not craggy and splendid, seamed with caves and tunnels, where the British garrison held out for so many months in a tawny-brown, waterless waste. Even farther beyond the town, the cemeteries for the war dead have a power not exerted by the living Tobruk. There are those for the French and the Italians, lying on opposite sides of the harbour mouth. But the most extensive are the German and the British, not far from each other at the beginning of the long drive to Jaghbub. The Germans built not a cemetery but a castle: a four-towered, blank, inward-turning fortress, standing above the new oil terminal of Marsa Harega. Here the whole concept is theatrical in what seems to be a German Expressionist way, with a sense of darkness, brooding stone, a great iron staircase soaring up to the unseen light; and round the courtyard towards which everything turns, a succession of walls on which the names of the dead run on continuously in mosaic, so that one wall blurs into a solid mass of Schmidts, another of Grubers. Here the dead seem regimented into one body, the Afrika Korps, with no room for individuality. Stone, iron and sun fuse into one solid and inhuman artefact.

In contrast, the British (or Commonwealth) cemetery is like a cottage-garden transplanted to the desert. 'Cottage' is right: the entrance to the cemetery has buildings which one has seen before, in England, as 'cottage hospitals' of the nineteen-twenties, cosy, small and snug-roomed, with sunny limestone and geraniums. Beyond it, 2,476 individual headstones fan out in neatly ordered rows, each with its name, rank, nationality: nationality, because not only Englishmen are buried here but Canadians, Australians, New Zealanders, South Africans, Indians, East and West Africans, men from the Seychelles and the Sudan, Czechs, French, Greeks, Poles, and many Libyans who served with the Senussi force – those, in fact, who made up the enormous polyglot army which the British somehow welded together in the early nineteen-forties. The order and tidiness of this place is unique in Libya, a world away from the desecrated and neglected Italian cemeteries in Cyrene and Benghazi, from the anonymous Muslim cairns of the desert, from the faceless citadel of the Afrika Korps. It seems to have nothing to do with its surroundings, but is an alien acreage of sentiment and patriotism flowering exotically, yet gently, in an unregarding land.

The King's own favourite palace (though that is too grand a word) is near Tobruk, and nowadays he seldom visits Jaghbub or anywhere else. He is old and frail. This palace of Dar-es-Salaam (the House of Peace) is efficiently run by the Queen, an Egyptian much younger than Idris, with an emancipated taste in fashions from Rome and Paris. It was the Queen who saw to it that the palace was furnished with modern Swedish chairs and tables and beds, rather than the tasteless gilt, glass and marble stuff that one finds in most rich Libyans' houses. The King himself, though still a powerful presence in the political life of the country, has never taken a direct and vigorous role in open policy-making, preferring to make the decisions quietly behind the scenes. And as time has gone on, he has more and more withdrawn from any semblance of political activity. In many ways he is probably out of touch. A British diplomat, visiting Dar-es-Salaam for the first time, told me the story of the King gravely asking after the health and welfare of the Prince of Wales. The diplomat began to speak about his successful school career at Gordonstoun and the plans for his undergraduate programme at Cambridge, and it was not until he noticed a look of incomprehension on the King's face that he realized the question related to that Prince of Wales who is now the Duke of Windsor – a royal personage whom the King had last met on some round-the-world tour in the 1920s.

The age and frailness of the King are so well known now that they are taken for granted: they were the excuses given for his absence from the 1967 Arab summit conference in Khartoum, for example, and no one in Libya any longer expects him to open the *Majlis*, or indeed ever to appear in public – though he did make one brief appearance in 1966 when he inaugurated the new oil terminal at Marsa Harega near Tobruk. I once saw him myself, on the road near Bomba where I was camping for the night: a 3-ton lorry of the Cyrenaican Defence Force had pulled off the road near me, and when I asked what was happening the driver told me that the King was expected during the next half-hour. After a little longer than that, there was a wailing of sirens in the distance, and there came into sight a procession of some twenty vehicles, including police and Cydef Land-Rovers, the King's personal ambulance, a whole retinue of black Mercedes, and the King himself momentarily glimpsed as a pale, white-bearded figure, hand raised in acknowledgement, sinking back on a mound of cushions in the car. He must have been returning from one of his rare visits to Tripoli, a journey he always makes by road – at very fast speeds – since he refuses to fly. Whenever stretches of the coastal road are repaired, it is said to be by order of the King; though his frail old body must have been sorely bruised and shaken sometimes along that grinding journey from Tripoli to Tobruk and back.

Idris has no children of his own, and his heir is his nephew, Crown Prince Hasan el-Rida, a man who is widely supposed – even by loyal Cyrenaicans – to be colourless, a mere cipher operated by his uncle and the royal household. 'The man without a shadow', they call him, because his personality is supposed to be so null. I've heard those who know the Crown Prince call this an unfair judgement, but the point is that it is the current coin in Libya. And even those who see him as a stronger personality than many give him credit for have to admit that his view of the world is limited and his ignorance sometimes frightening. But Hasan el-Rida's capabilities are neither here nor there. For reasons of history and sentiment, Idris has a loyal following; Hasan has no history, no sentimental following. It may be that his accession will mean a split between a Cyrenaican monarchy and a Tripolitanian republic. This could involve civil war – and it is here, of course, that the danger of Egypt on the eastern frontier shows itself most clearly; the danger too, perhaps, of Algeria to the west. Both countries would badly like to control Libyan oil, and one is aware that 'peace and stability' would be easily operated slogans with which to mask a takeover in Libya if civil war broke out between Tripolitanians and Cyrenaicans, or between royalists and republicans. Here would be an ideal opportunity for either, or both, to step in, with the excuse that only they could restore order and give stable government. Idris is well aware of the dangers of such poaching: in a speech to the people several years ago, on the occasion of the annual December independence celebrations, he said: 'The difficulty of gaining our independence is as nothing to the difficulty of keeping it.'

Political parties were abolished at an early stage in Libya's independent history, after some fierce factional struggles between members of Tripolitanian nationalist groups. There are still, very broadly, some 'opposition' figures about on the scene, but since political alignments are so obscure it is difficult to see quite what they are opposed to. Mustafa Baiou, Rector of the University when I first arrived, and later Minister of Education, is such a figure, and in his case perhaps all that is meant by 'opposition' is that he is a forceful individualist, unafraid of dubious subjects and unpopular attitudes. Immediately after the Israeli victory in June 1967, Baiou was walking down Istiklal, the main street in Benghazi, when he saw a group of university students on the pavement, lounging about and chatting. The examinations hadn't yet been resumed after the sudden cancellation, but Baiou would hardly take this for an excuse. He went up to the group and publicly denounced them for wasting their own and their country's time: 'You know why Israel has won? Because everyone, every man and woman, every student, has worked hard. Go back to your books!' The students slunk away.

'Why worry? We have oil' is perhaps not as common an attitude as one might expect, and it doesn't account by itself for idleness and lack of ambition, wherever one finds them. But it is oil that lies most crucially under whatever stage Libya has now reached. However ancient Libya's history, however traditional its basic ways, oil has forced history and tradition to be assessed and judged radically.

The biggest oil strikes have been made in Cyrenaica, though recently more success than was expected result came Tripolitanian exploration. The largest and most productive of the lot is Zelten, run by Esso, which is reached along a road specially built by the company, a hundred miles due south of Marsa Brega, the terminal of the pipeline and the loading port for the tankers. Using this road is the easiest way to reach the desert from the coast. But that needs some qualification. The word *desert* suggests to most people limitless quantities of sand, or – more vaguely – a void with a floor to it. But it is a relative term: one man's desert is another man's pre-desert, and some will find the fourteen miles between Benghazi and Benina Airport enough of a desert to bear. The Calanscio Sand Sea, which begins within sight of Jaghbub and then rolls on south towards Tchad for hundreds of miles, is the 'classic' desert: a mass of shifting dunes, unstable as waves, blown into tall ridges which run north and south because of the previling winds. The desert between Marsa Brega and Zelten is not like that. Instead, there is a surprising solidity about the landscape. The long straight Esso road, a ribbon of efficient tarmac, moves through a country untouched by anything but the sun and the wind. The tall rocks seem to fountain and feather in the air, worn by the hot sand-laden wind. It seems like Grand

Canyon without the tourists, vistas of rock rather than sand. The desert floor is firm in patches, covered where it is firm with fossil shells, hard black gobbets of crude oil, and twisted pieces of metal which at first I took to be fragments of meteorite, then shrapnel, but eventually tracked down in Tripoli Museum as 'silicaceous arenaria concretions' – stones which had been twisted and rubbed until they showed what is called 'desert varnish', the result of driving sand at high speed, a sort of natural polishing device.

On the road from Marsa Brega to Zelten there is nothing but the pipeline stretching along beside it: at one point, an empty oil-drum is topped with a battered sign pointing to Gialo, far along difficult tracks. Marsa Brega, on the coast, is an alien outpost, where Esso have built a whole self-contained and self-sufficient community for their employees. It is like an American suburb plonked down on the shores of North Africa, with school, church, community centre, family houses, and familiar foods. But Zelten is no such settlement: its object is work, and there are no families or frills there. At the end of the hot drive down, I walked with a friend into the Nissen-type hut which serves as a clubroom for the bachelors, or temporary bachelors, who run the oil installations. As we walked in, friendly but without ostentation, we saw that the whole room was lined with men slumped in armchairs. No one was reading, or talking, or doing anything other than staring into space. I asked whether we could buy a drink, and after a few moments' pause one man indicated with his hand a door on the far side. Through it, we found a water-cooler. And that was that. No word of greeting – indeed, no word at all – was exchanged. It seemed like a dreadful static mime of desert *cafard*. I never went back to Zelten again.

But the first view of Zelten, lying at the bottom of steeply descending weathered ridges, is a fine one: the oily flames flare against the clear blue sky, swirling with black smoky edges, and obscuring the mean hutments and the rather unimpressive externals of an oil-rig. Beyond it the purer desert begins, but almost nowhere now is really untouched, for the geologists in their Land-Rovers have covered the bleakest and most remote stretches in their search for oil. This desert has never blossomed like the rose and never will. But in a sense it is of course richer and more productive than anywhere else in Libya. It is the Cyrenaican

✳ 118

coast that is barren, yielding nothing but poor dates, feeble barley, dry scrub for goats and donkeys. The 'black gold' has made the Libyan desert the deserts of Hesperides, a jealously guarded zone of magical properties. Multi-purpose silphium – the umbelliferous plant-panacea, now apparently extinct, which was one of Cyrenaica's chief exports for centuries – gives way to multi-purpurpose petroleum. Silphium could not, and oil cannot, be a panacea. But for the time being, the desert is yielding one of the richest cash crops in the world.

7 · Treasures in Grenna

WHEN the Delphic Oracle launched the first wave of Greek colonists into Libya in about the middle of the seventh century B.C., she did so with the words: 'Battus, thou camest to ask for a voice, but the Lord Apollo sendeth thee to found a city in Libya, which giveth good pasture to sheep.' For Battus, who came from the small, barren Aegean island of Thera (the modern Santorin), had come to seek a cure for his appalling stammer. To be asked to found a city in unknown Africa was puzzling; but the Oracle's replies were always puzzling, so Battus duly did as he was told.

But the first settlement was not on the mainland. A small rocky island, one of three off the coast near Bomba, seems to have been temporarily occupied, but which of the three isn't certain. Herodotus calls it Platea. Then there is evidence for a mainland settlement – earlier than that at Cyrene – on the coast east of Derna, given by Herodotus as Aziris, but again there is much hypothesis with little to show for it. What Herodotus goes on to tell seems borne out by archaeological evidence – that Cyrene was founded in about 630 B.C. – but of course there is no way of testing his account of how the Greeks under Battus got there. 'The Libyans,' he writes, 'undertook to show them a better place. After getting them to consent to move, the Libyans took them farther west, and so timed the journey to pass through the finest bit of country – called Irasa – in the dark, in order to prevent them from seeing it. Finally they reached the spring called Apollo's Fountain, and the Libyan guides said to the Greeks: "This is the place for you to settle in, for here there is a hole in the sky."' Was the ambiguity intended? Did the Libyans simply mean that the rain is heavy, which it is, or that to be here was to be nearer the gods?

Whichever they meant, here the Greeks settled. When Paolo della Cella, the physician to the Bey of Tripoli and a keen if slovenly antiquarian, passed through in 1817, the Bey accosted him with the words: 'You Christians have all the same passion for hunting after and examining all the old dilapidated buildings in my father's dominions; but, tell me truly, have you discovered any treasures in Grenna?' (Grenna being the Arabic name for the ruins of Cyrene.) Della Cella sensibly didn't try to impress the Bey with statues or mosaics, but instead led him to 'a most valuable treasure – a spring of delicious water issuing from the mountains, and sufficiently copious to supply the wants not only of your whole army, but of all the Bedouins and their flocks which follow you'. This was the Fountain of Apollo. But for the 'ruin-bibber, randy for antique' there are indeed treasures in Grenna, in a setting incomparable (in my experience) in the ancient world, beyond Leptis Magna and the Valley of the Kings; more like Delphi, but still finer.

Cyrene is built on the edge of a steep escarpment, the second step of the Jebel Akhdar. It is a hill-top city, reaching up to its Acropolis like Athens, and landscaped in such a way that the first impression is of tier after tier of walls and columns, a hanging garden of ruins. In the distance to the north is the sea, lying below the steep first step of the Jebel, sometimes so blurred with cloud or heat-haze that you cannot tell where sky ends and sea begins. And the plain below is deeply shadowed with wadis, narrow and plunging valleys covered with stunted junipers and oleanders, with the tumbled white rocks at the bottom stained red by the ochreous earth.

The air at Cyrene, even in the hottest days of summer, is clear, clean, and fragrant with pine and juniper smells. Hawks hang above the escarpment, wheeling and swooping, sometimes alone, sometimes in squadrons of dozens; they seem like guardians of the Necropolis, the great settlement of ancient tombs which is Cyrene's strangest and most impressive feature. Because the shelly, yellowish-white limestone is soft and easy to carve, like Bath stone, the hillsides and wadis on all sides below the Acropolis became over the centuries a warren of rock-cut tombs, shafts cut horizontally into the face of the land, each with its niches for votive statuary and funerary lamps, some with elaborately carved lintels and panels in imitation of wood. Then there are the free-standing graves – the hog-backed sarcophagi, and the circular and rectangular tombs, some of them intended for multiple interments and as big as temples. In this city of the dead there are over two

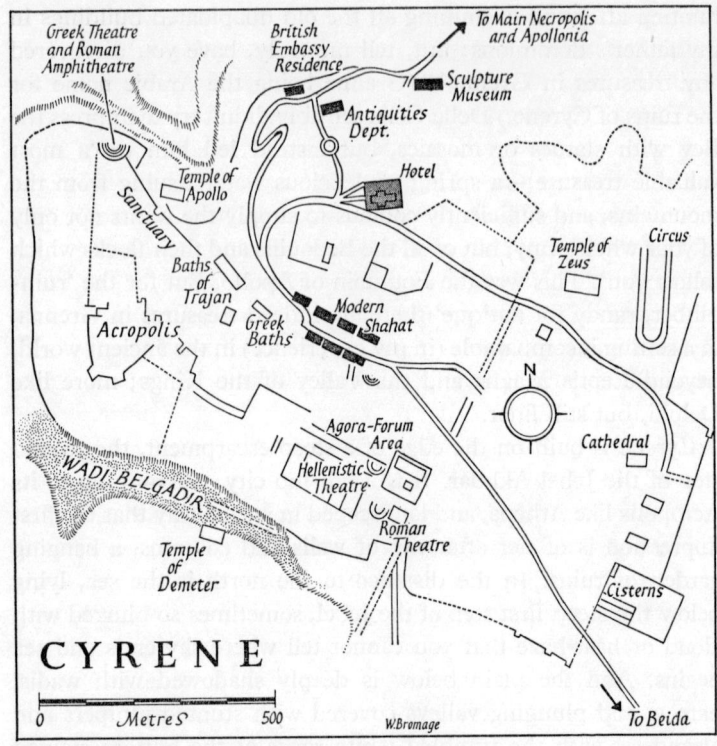

Greek Theatre
and Roman
Amphitheatre

British
Embassy
Residence

To Main Necropolis
and Apollonia

Sculpture
Museum

Antiquities
Dept.

Temple of
Apollo

Hotel

Sanctuary

Baths
of
Trajan

Temple of
Zeus

Circus

Acropolis

Greek
Baths

Modern
Shahat

N

WADI BELGADIR

Agora-Forum
Area

Cathedral

Hellenistic
Theatre

Temple
of
Demeter

Roman
Theatre

Cisterns

CYRENE

0   Metres   500   W.Bromage   To Beida

thousand sarcophagi alone, and so many rock-cut tombs that
when you come up the circuitous modern road from Apollonia
in the late afternoon as the sun is throwing its last light on the
hillside, the slopes are pock-marked with holes of darkness. Later,
lights here and there show you that many of the tombs are
inhabited; in the often bitter winter weather of the Jebel, and in
rain (for Cyrene has the highest rainfall in Libya), they are warm
and dry, and to live in them is not considered a sign of poverty or
shameful. When Graziani was governor of Cyrenaica, he tried to
evict all the tomb-dwellers so that Cyrene could be purely a
zona archaeologica, but his efforts were unsuccessful, and though
the Libyan government still occasionally murmurs about re-
housing them no one seems much convinced. A few of the tombs
which have traces of wall-painting or particularly fine carvings
have been fitted with locked gates by the Antiquities Department
(from whom visitors may ask for keys), but most of them are

either tidily whitewashed and lived in or have been abandoned to goats, cattle, bees and fleas.

In age the majority range from the fourth century B.C. to Hellenistic and Roman times: some are as early as sixth century B.C., some as late as Byzantine. They normally belonged to families, and the bigger of them have shelf-room for five, six, or even more bodies. The characteristic guardian of these tombs was the mourning figure of a woman, sometimes three-quarter length but often simply a head and shoulders with one hand held to the face. But 'face' gives the wrong impression, for many of these figures are quite deliberately faceless: 'aniconic' is the correct term. Above the naturalistically carved drapery and hand, a smooth polished cone stares sightlessly out – the blank face of death, it's tempting to say, though John Cassels's theory* is that a real veil of woven material covered the face, suspended from a disc on top of the head and completely masking the area where the features should be. None of these so-called Persephone figures remains *in situ*, but in and around the Sculpture Museum they are ranged like monitory presences.

This setting of the Necropolis is as theatrical as anything the Italians might have hoped for in their twentieth-century planning of Libya: the whole side of the escarpment turned north-east to meet the sun as it rises, and the empty honeycomb of dark tombs – all of them a solid contrast with the impermanent Muslim graves one sees everywhere in Libya, which are mere scratchings in the surface sand, bones hurried into shallow graves below untidy cairns that sometimes seem no more than the sweepings of a field. They are a contrast, too, with the Italian cemetery at Cyrene, which even more than its equivalent in Benghazi is pitiful in its waste and desecration: most of the graves belonged to soldiers fighting in the Senussi wars, and there is not one of them that remains unspoiled. The most conspicuous monument of all is a column erected by the colonists of Sousa in memory of the Askari troops who fought in Cyrenaica – those black Christians from Eritrea and Somaliland who were particularly hated by the Arabs; they wore huge silver crosses on cords round their necks, and were the particular pride of Graziani, who said to them (in a

* 'The Cemeteries of Cyrene': *Papers of the British School at Rome* (Vol. XXIII – New Series, Vol. X, 1955).

speech made in Benghazi in 1930): 'New battles lie before you, but I know that you will be victorious together with us Italians, who profess the same religion as you.' Their Cyrene column is split down the middle, a mark of exuberant revenge. But even before this happened, presumably in 1941, the Libyans had had a first taste of revenge: in the Abysinnian campaigns of 1935, a volunteer force of Libyans was raised to join the Italian army, and proved surprisingly popular: they were glad to get their own back against the Ethiopians, whom they identified with the Eritreans, for both were black Christians. One of the clerks in the University Library in Benghazi was a boy-soldier in Abysinnia with this Libyan detachment; he was wounded in an engagement and managed to sham dead, lying face down in a river, while the Ethiopians swarmed over him. Some Libyans still have their Italian campaign medals for their part in this war, and are proud of them.

As at Leptis and Sabratha, the chief credit for the restoration of Cyrene as it can be seen today must go to the Italians, though the first scientific excavations were carried out there, immediately before the Italian occupation, by an American expedition in 1910: the grave of one of them, Herbert De Cou, lies above the road near the main entrance to the ruins – 'the victim', as a later American archaeologist laconically put it, 'of a disaffected tribesman's bullet'. Fifty years earlier, in 1860, two Englishmen, R. M. Smith and E. A. Porcher, dug at Cyrene and secured over 150 pieces of sculpture, which are now in the British Museum. But it was the discovery of the so-called 'Venus of Cyrene', brought to light in a torrential rainstorm in the winter of 1913, that spurred the Italians into starting work, and in particular the fifteen years before the Second World War saw an effort of scholarship, labour and money which equalled the efforts at Leptis and Sabratha.

But Cyrene is an altogether more confusing site than either of the Tripolitanian cities, for the span of its existence was much longer, and consequently the archaeologists and restorers were faced with the ruins of buildings of many different periods, many of which would not have co-existed in antiquity. Thus the Baths of Trajan and the Byzantine Baths that succeeded them lie close to one another, and near by is the fourth century B.C. Strategheion, a war-treasury which was later repaired in the early Roman period.

Such juxtapositions mean that one gets little sense of a functioning and living city, as one does at Leptis.

It is better, perhaps, not to attempt to reconstruct such a city as one walks about Cyrene, but in any case the right place to begin, both chronologically and aesthetically, is the Fountain and Shrine of Apollo, the cause itself for Cyrene being founded where it was. For Kurana, a Greek nymph whom Apollo pursued and brought to Libya, was the tutelary spirit of Cyrene, and from her the city took its Greek name, Kurene, of which the modern English and Italian names are simply corruptions. The Fountain itself is a spring gushing out from the rock face, having its source deep in the hillside. It flows out into rock-cut basins and troughs, but nowadays the main force of the water is deliberately blocked so as to provide enough for the modern village of Shahat, which straggles along a road lined with imported eucalyptus trees: it's sometimes hard to imagine that the eucalyptus, which now seems so much a native of the Mediterranean, was until the 1880s exclusively an Australian tree, and was planted in Libya on a large scale by the Italian colonists, partly for its mosquito-repellent qualities.

Below the high rock face, incised and shaped so that it is a cunning blend of natural form and man-made architecture, stand the ruins of the Temple of Apollo, the foundations of which are of the sixth century B.C., though the tall Doric columns which mark it now were not put up until the second century A.D. Close by is a fountain, the water of which flows through a stone lion's mouth; and the athletic Kurana forms part of the composition as she strangles the lion – this being the masculine feat which enticed Apollo into carrying her off. There are many representations of this lion-taming act recorded at Cyrene, for example on the coins of the city, and it formed part of the 'image' (as we might say now) of the place, which was often described by ancient writers as 'eminent in games'. Certainly it seems to have won a fair proportion of prizes in the Panathenaic Games, if one can judge by the number of Panathenaic vases recorded as found in the area: these were huge red-figure urns, inscribed as presentation cups are today, and very highly valued as sports trophies. Pindar in his Odes praised the Cyrenean athletes. Though such skill has hardly yet had a chance to develop in modern Libya, there was a new Cabinet appointment in 1967, in the person of a Minister of Youth and Sport; and Benghazi has been chosen as the site for the next Pan-Arab Games. It would be fitting if Libya managed to get a team – and a successful one – together for the next Olympic Games: given the right incentive, a Cyrenaican Bedouin might easily win one of the walking races, judging from the long, inexorable pace they can keep up on their desert treks.

On the same level as Apollo's Fountain and Sanctuary there is a large theatre of the Greek period, converted into an amphitheatre for wild animals and gladiators in Roman times: though much less restored than those at Leptis and Sabratha, it gives one of the best views of Cyrene, looking out across the plain hundreds of feet below, with the Mediterranean and the brilliant blue sky as a natural backdrop. But not always a brilliant blue sky, for the clouds pile up above Cyrene often, even in summer, and confirm the truth of the 'hole in heaven' recommendation. The wind can be fierce, too, and snow sometimes falls in winter, though it seldom settles. Whenever I suggested to Libyans that Cyrene would have made an excellent site for the University of Libya, being redolent with the right associations as well as being more beautiful and healthier than Benghazi, the reaction was always that it was far too cold. Even on a warm summer day Shahat is full of men thickly bundled up with sweaters and greatcoats.

On top of the slope behind the Sanctuary are the Agora, what remains of the Acropolis buildings (now largely confused by an Italian fort and defensive walls), and a whole complex of buildings leading to two more theatres and the Forum. It was in a pine-grove opposite the Forum that we parked and camped on our first visit, waking to see the dawn coming up appropriately, for a predominantly Greek city, 'rosy-fingered'. The scent of the pines has a cool sharpness which one misses in the more pungent and less easily distinguishable smells of the plain: here one can precisely pick out eucalyptus, juniper, and the deeper smell of earth and damp vegetation rather than the thin, dry, throat-caking sensation of sand. The floor of the Forum is thick with wild flowers in spring, and good barley is grown on the slopes to the south, right up to the Italian wall which acts as a demarcation on that side for the Antiquities Department site. On these slopes I found coins, and some good pieces of pottery, after ploughing –

often done here by camels, which at all times of the year browse on the upper levels at Cyrene. The land then plunges sharply down to the Wadi Belgadir, the far side of which is seamed with rock-cut tombs which run in an almost continuous band, like a row of portholes.

The village of Shahat, the village that lies in the middle of Cyrene, is an entirely modern creation, most of it dating from the early years of the Italian occupation. There is a monstrous hotel, where Mussolini stayed in 1937: it has cavernous rooms, much bilious coloured glass, and an ornamental glass fountain in the foyer in the conventionalized shape of a silphium plant. The whole construction shows Fascist architecture at its worst. Yet it is not a bad place at which to stay, if the present management still remains – a Lebanese married to an Englishwoman – and the view from its terrace, overlooking the distant coastal plain through pine trees, is splendid. The guests are usually government officials and others with business in Beida, such as Turkish cultural delegations and dignified Moroccan *imams*.

Below the level of the hotel are the museum – well-stocked but shabby – and the library and offices of the Antiquities Department; we stayed for a time in the guest-rooms of the Department, which are round the back of the sculpture museum, and in fact connect in an odd fashion with the exhibition rooms. We had the use of a primitive kerosene cooker, but were asked not to cook during the day, as the fumes and smells would drift into the museum over the top of the partition. But the museum is in any case little visited.

Close to the Antiquities buildings is the Cyrene British Embassy residence, the former country seat of Graziani, who built himself what was described to me as a 'funk-hole' underneath it – a bomb-proof shelter, now blocked up at both entrances. The Jebel Akhdar was the centre of Senussi resistance to the Italians, right up to Omar Mukhtar's death, and no Italian could have felt safe there until the 'pacification' was complete.

Below the main road of modern Shahat the ancient 'valley street' runs between the Baths of Trajan and the Greek Baths, which lie behind the high wall of the Sacred Way: you have to climb over this wall at one of its lower levels to reach them. These rock-cut baths are some of the most extraordinary things at Cyrene.

Chambers have been cut deep in the rock-face, and each chamber is lined with rows of what Goodchild calls 'sitz baths': niches big enough for a seated person, and above them smaller niches for lamps and water jars. Because of the filling-in of the valley at the time of the building of the Sacred Way in the second century A.D., the baths are obscurely lit from the outside world, and the stone is everywhere green and almost luminous with mould. How they were used is unknown: in some moods, the theory that they were ritual baths for the dedication of girls to Artemis is tempting, and on the wall of the Antiquities Department there hangs a framed feature from the *Illustrated London News* showing a reconstruction of the supposed ceremonies that went with this – lightly-clothed maidens undergoing a kind of orgiastic purification. On the other hand, less fanciful eyes may turn them into a row of purely functional bidets. Whatever they were, their present darkness and mysteriousness seem, however unjustifiably, part of the arcane atmosphere of the whole Sanctuary area.

The unexcavated ruins of Cyrene lie all along the road towards the modern Derna/Beida cross-roads, and any trench- or foundation-digging turns up something. When the new secondary school was being built a few years ago, the contractors came across a hoard of archaic Greek statuary and metal objects, including a huge bronze platter whose top surface was a Gorgon head: this was being reassembled, partly in the Antiquities Department workshops and partly in America, from hundreds of fragments of corroded green bronze. And local farmers are always handing in coins they pick up while ploughing, for which the Department pays a standard rate of £1 for silver and £5 for gold. Because no tourist and souvenir industry has sprung up at Cyrene, the Cyrenaican Department has an easier job than some in its acquisition of such things: one day I was in Awad Sadawiya's office when one of the inspectors, Abdul-karim Mayar, brought in a graceful marble hand, clutching a fragment of fluted drapery, which had been found by a farmer in a wadi bed near Apollonia. It had been stained red by the earth, and from the break at the wrist looked as if it had been deliberately mutilated by some zealot during the Christian period, when many of the pagan statues in Cyrenaica were smashed and burnt in the lime-kilns. Even later, under the Arabs, much marble was used from the statues and the facings of buildings, as a good ingredient in potter's clay: early Arab pottery often contains fine chips and marble powder. Stephen Levinson, who was helping in the Department the summer before he went up to Cambridge, found a beautifully sculpted marble finger on the slope leading down towards the Wadi Belgadir, which was bigger than life-size and might even have come from the huge statues that were destroyed in the Temple of Zeus. A patina of lime and other mineral deposits had formed along the knuckle, but the nail was still cleanly cut and gleaming white.

The Temple of Zeus was the largest temple in Cyrene – bigger than the Parthenon in Athens and the Temple of Zeus at Olympia. Like so many building in Cyrene, it had been destroyed and rebuilt more than once: certainly in the Jewish revolt of A.D. 115, and again by an earthquake in A.D. 365. It was after this earthquake that the local Christians wrecked what survived, and the ruins as they now are seem like the result of titanic havoc. But the Italians before the war re-erected just one of the colossal Doric columns, to show what the effect must have been like when these giant drums stood over thirty feet high. The others lie along the sides of the temple, fallen and shattered like the bones of some dinosaur. The marble feet, almost all that remains of the seated statue of Zeus which originally was placed at the far end of the temple's interior, are in the Sculpture museum; and they show that the figure was twelve times life size. The fallen Rameses at Thebes is the only thing I have ever seen which could match it in its Ozymandias-like degradation.

But vandalism is not only a thing of the past in Cyrenaica. Although the farmers have responded well enough to the Antiquities Department's wheedlings over handing in found antiquities, the biggest menace is other government departments and government contractors, who are frequently bulldozing and wrecking. Sadawiya, the Cyrenaican Controller, has a constant battle: in the past few years *gsur* near Beida and Suani Tika and Greek tombs near Messa have been demolished, and all that the Department can hope to do is to bring in delaying actions until at least the better things are saved. But such speed carries its own dangers, in an accumulation of hastily excavated objects which lie at Cyrene until someone expert enough can find the time to catalogue and preserve them. A magnificent Panathenaic vase rescued from a tomb near Beida, for example, was rapidly crumbling and flaking away in a cardboard box, along with a great heap of less distinguished pottery, until Stephen Levinson found it and made a preservative restoration. Most Libyans, often even intelligent ones, have no interest whatever in their Graeco-Roman antiquities. I'm reminded of a story one of the English V.S.O.s told me soon after his arrival for a year's service in Derna. He was given a lift from Beida to Derna in a big Mercedes, and it turned out that the man who had picked him up was a senior Libyan official. The boy excitedly pointed out, and exclaimed at, the ruins which line the route to left and right much of the way. Apparently wearied by this, the civil servant waved away such antiquarian enthusiasm with: 'Yes, yes, we have many of them, too many. I wish they would all sink into the ground.'

The road that runs the eleven miles from Cyrene to Apollonia is one of the most beautiful (as well as one of the best-surfaced) in Libya. For some of the way it follows the line of the ancient route, but at times it takes spectacular hairpin bends and leaps that only modern engineering could have achieved, while the old road can be seen hugging the edge of the hill above you. This was the road until the late 1930s, when the Via Balbo and its subsidiaries were built. If the Italians did nothing else in Libya, they at least did the basic pioneering on the country's network of roads, and some of their achievements – the Garian pass, the Tocra pass, the Apollonia road – have been well preserved and renewed.

The final descent from the first step of the Jebel to the plain gives a panoramic view of Apollonia, stretched out along the coast below. More obvious is the modern village of Sousa, founded by Cretan Muslims in the 1890s and much developed by the Italians. But Sousa today is a depressing place, and one of the few in Libya where one is pursued by children asking for *bakshish* – often children whose lighter hair and blue eyes show that they are still much more Cretan than Arab. Greek is often spoken within the family. But there is nothing Greek in spirit about the place itself. The Italians built the place into what must have been superficially a thriving community, but their departure left a legacy of decaying bungalows, boarded-up churches, and collapsing public buildings. As on the slopes near El Abiar, or in the rich valleys south of

Teknis, or – most extensively – on the Barce plain, one is reminded how much the Italians (self-seeking and ruthless, admittedly) did to develop Libya, and how utterly their work has been neglected and destroyed: Bayyada, Farzugha, Oelia, and the mile after mile of regularly plotted white farmhouses stretching away from the road between Barce and Tolmeita – all bear out Gwyn Williams's remark that 'Libya is a land where ruins flourish'. Leptis Magna, Sabratha, Cyrene, Apollonia, Tocra, Tolmeita are followed by D'Annunzio, Maddalena, Luigi di Savoia, Marconi, Crispi . . . The goat returns, and the Bedouin: imperturbable, building nothing, staying nowhere, ignoring agricultural research stations, horticultural institutes and government rhetoric. Such reflections come too easily to a settled man, whether English, Russian or Japanese, and such people can seldom make the imaginative leap necessary to take the Bedouin for what he is and not something else – for he is not a failed farmer or a failed townsman; he is native, he is what survives.

There is good swimming off the road to Apollonia, and it was here on the beach one day that we were joined by a large family of Libyans, who from the start were enormously friendly, and also very free among themselves. One middle-aged woman stripped off her upper gaments and went into the sea with naked breasts and great flounces of dress billowing round her waist. All the women were tattooed, and the children were bright and eager. The husband of one of the women told me they all came from Benghazi, and that he worked for the Banco di Roma there – most likely as a watchman, I thought. They had much more the open air of country people, without that stifling formality and closeness which seems to go so often with town-dwellers in Cyrenaica – a relic of the Turkish occupation, which imported the whole *harem* concept into the country, with its idle, captive women, its veiling, its surreptitiousness. That day near Apollonia there were no such restrictions. We took photographs of one another, and our children splashed in the sea together, until a lorry came down the track to take the family back to Benghazi.

Apollonia was the port of Cyrene for over a thousand years, and more than any other ancient site in Libya it is dominated by the sea – dominated and partly subjugated, for perhaps half the town lies under the waves. Swimming underwater here is exciting, where storage chambers and rock-cut channels loom through the clear green water, thronged with bright pebbles, fish, and waving ferny sea-plants. There has been some official underwater exploration by the British, but nothing has yet been done on a scale sufficient to make more than tentative plans of what parts of Apollonia are submerged. The most impressive remains are of the three churches and the Byzantine Governor's Palace: here it is possible to drive almost on to the beach, where in the low cliff face I found a tiny scrap of pottery with a perfect red-figure profile of a youth, his long nose, huge doe-like eye and tight curls as fresh as the day he was made. Such classical features seemed right for Apollonia, where the local Antiquities Inspector is a delightful man of Cretan descent, with a quite un-Arab face, stance, informality, and vivaciousness. He has made a garden round the small museum at the western end of the ruins, where he plucked some geraniums and gave them to the children.

The theatre, which lies to the east just on the far side of the Hellenistic city walls, is the best preserved in Cyrenaica, though the restorer's hand has been a bit heavy in places. But the setting, right on the edge of the sea, is superb, and the crash of the waves on the rocks beyond the *orchestra* is dramatic – though in a way not intended, for the stage wall that originally stood behind it has gone, and the coast has sunk since ancient times, so that in fact the acoustics have been changed out of all recognition. It's tempting to think of this stage as possibly having seen a production of *The Rope* by Plautus, for the action of the play is set on the sea-shore near Cyrene, and it would have thus a local relevance and bite – like seeing *Hamlet* at Elsinore.

The coast road between Apollonia and Derna is narrow and often twisting as it negotiates the wadis, where the bridges are sometimes washed away by the force of the torrents in winter and spring: one bridge was out of action for the whole of our two years in Cyrenaica, and this meant driving hard in low gear to plunge down one side of the wadi and up the other side to reach the road again. But there are fine steep rocky coves and bays all along the seaward side, floored with large white pebbles and sometimes riddled with caves. At Ras el Hilal a promontory sticks out into the sea, forming a natural breakwater to the east: there is deep water here, and below the level of the cliff the Italians built

Two views of Cyrene

Sabratha, the theatre
*Photograph courtesy Radio
Times Hulton Picture Library*

Fred's funeral, 1 June 1967

Lucy, Caroline, Alice and
Emily *Photograph by
Roloff Beny*

rock-cut submarine pens, reached above ground by a track which leads through a cliff tunnel. Now there is a jetty there, used by the Libyan Customs launch, its officials dressed in very natty naval uniform. Libya is hardly naval-minded, despite the purchase from Britain a few years ago of a corvette and the training of some cadets at Dartmouth. When in 1959 the International Bank for Reconstruction and Development prepared a report on the economic development of Libya, one of their recommendations was that this harbour at Ras el Hilal should be fitted to act as a landing-station for tourists on Mediterranean cruises, who would thereby much more handily reach Apollonia and Cyrene than overland from Benghazi: the cost of repairing the concrete jetty and making a turning place for buses was estimated then at £30,000, not a large figure when set against the total budget for tourism; but the recommendation was not taken up, and probably never will be. Meanwhile Ras el Hilal is the more peaceful.

The village-centre of Ras el Hilal, like that of Jedida near Tocra, is one of the five resettlement projects set up by the Italians for the Libyans between 1936 and 1942. Unlike Jedida, it was actually fully functioning for a time, but today it has little more to show than a dry fountain, a few shuttered white buildings, a mosque, and a couple of shops which serve as general stores for the area, selling the typical Cyrenaican mixture of tomato paste, bread, fizzy orange drinks, torch batteries, and cigarettes. The whole concept is beautiful but wrong – an Italian *piazza* artificially created in the middle of an alien country and an alien tradition. Even so, its immediate effect of tidy white symmetry has been enough for it to be the subject of postcards and illustrated 'literature' whenever the Department of Tourism has put its mind to publicizing the delights of Libya. The only trouble is that it's no more typical of Cyrenaica than any other relic of the Italian occupation.

Just on the other side of Ras el Hilal is a bumpy track leading off to the right, marked at the main road by a small Byzantine column. Up here is the house and farm of Miss Brittan, the most celebrated Englishwoman in Libya, bee-keeper and honey-supplier to King Idris, and a notable figure in her own right. It would be hard, if not impertinent, to guess Olive Brittan's age, but she must be at least sixty, though when we swam with her in

✳ 133

the little cove at Ain Treitish near by she was as vigorous as anyone half that age. She was advising the Jordanian government, and keeping bees, in the 1950s, when King Idris sampled her honey while on a visit to Jordan; he was so taken with it and her that he invited her to Libya, where she has stayed ever since, nominally the responsibility of, and on the payroll of, the Department of Agriculture; but – as she never ceases to asseverate – she takes orders from no one but the King, or if vitally necessary the Prime Minister. She is a short, square, multi-garmented, indomitable figure, much given to bursts of invective against the rogues and scoundrels who harass her, bubbling over with exuberance and prejudice ('They've got spies on me now . . . That man Ali tried to shoot me again last week . . . What this country needs is a *Christian* archaeologist – we've never had one, they're all atheists . . . Synesius is buried at Ras el Hilal – I know it . . . I told the Under-Secretary that it was no good trying to budge me, I'll go straight to the King . . .'). She speaks fluent Arabic with an exaggeratedly English 'county' accent, and has no time for fools or idlers, most of whom seem to manage to get into the Department of Agriculture.

Her house is a big, bare, Italian farm, pre-ENTE colonization. On the walls are relics of wartime German occupation – caricatures of Churchill, idealized murals of pure Aryan German soldiers. Her honey is stacked up among gleaming metal equipment, each jar marked with its source and date: the King's favourite is apparently a clear light yellow, thin and delicious, which thickened creamily and satisfyingly in the refrigerator when we took it home. The whole of this wadi where Miss Brittan lives – the Wadi Glaa – is lush with vegetation: tall cultivated palms, figs, pomegranates, olives. On one visit we found that she wasn't at home but was off for the day collecting mud from Marawa for some mysterious apiary purpose. We walked over the bee-hill with one of her workers: a natural mound terraced with rocks, on each terrace a row of beehives – white boxes covered with straw. He showed us what he said was a Libyan beehive, to us not markedly different from the others, but no good according to the man: Miss Brittan's English beehives were the best. She is a great patriot, with framed portraits of the Queen and Prince Philip in her vast empty living-room.

※ 134

Later we were taken down to the arbour by the house, where we were given fat bunches of grapes plucked warm from the trellis. On the way down, the man hacked his way through the mass of jungly undergrowth, giving some creepers a vicious swipe with his stick and roaring 'Fucking bastard!' No doubt he had worked for the British army when there was a garrison at Derna, and was airing his command of the vernacular for our benefit. He grinned at my disconcerted look, loaded us with Miss Brittan's grapes, and unlocked the gates which barricade her track all the way up to the house. Embattled she may or may not be, but she certainly has spirit. Her house and her conversation are a favourite goal of the R.A.F. people at El Adhem (the last remaining British military base in Libya), whose presence along this coast – in the way of beer and orange-juice tins marked *NAAFI* – is contradictory testimony to those who say that the Libyans are worse at scattering litter than anyone else in the world.

Behind Miss Brittan's farm the wadi stretches up, running parallel below the road to Lamluda, to a waterfall, and beyond that (reachable by a track from the road, but only on foot) is an idyllic hollow where there is a clear, deep pool of fresh water, fed by the stream above which descends over worn rocks. All round are oleanders, myrtle, and juniper. Coming hot from the car one day, we swam there in the stingingly cold water, until a man approached us – politely, but to our horror – telling us that the pool was used for drinking water. We clambered out, chagrined, but glad to have had our swim first. On other visits we did see young men swimming there, so we were never sure how literally we were meant to take the advice. Below the pool women often wash and pummel their clothes on the flat rocks by the stream. In this sheltered, prolific hollow, it's difficult to imagine that one is in north Africa: the scrub country and the desert seem continents away, though in fact an hour's drive brings one to the desolate wastes south of the Ain Mara–Martuba road.

The road up to Lamluda passes close to four free-standing early Greek tombs, as big as any in the Cyrene necropolis, and better preserved than most. It's difficult to tell what settlement they were connected with, for Lamluda itself (the ancient Limnias) seems too far away, and anyway is largely of later Roman and Byzantine date. But Lamluda is a delightful site, compact and overgrown with trees and bushes in the angle between the main road to Derna and the secondary road to Ras el Hilal. Some of the biggest tortoises I've ever seen waddle about heavily in its ruins, and there is a fine vaulted church with solid fortifications. The whole of this stretch of main road between Lamluda and the Cyrene cross-roads is littered with ruins – arches, cisterns, tombs – including an Italian fort at Tert which is built out of, and on top of, a much earlier building, and a very long vaulted water cistern at Safsaf, where the modern road and the ancient one, deeply rutted in its white slabs, run side by side for about a hundred yards.

Labraq, just to the east of the Cyrene cross-roads, is the airport for Beida, inconveniently far away but chosen because there was an airstrip still existing from wartime which could be renovated. A number of British work as radio control officers and engineers there, though they could not apparently prevent a blunder so gross that I am still not sure whether to believe it or not: when the airport control tower was erected, everything about it was perfectly correct with one exception – it faced the wrong way. Still, a Kingdom of Libya Airlines service regularly shuttles between Benghazi and Labraq without serious mishap, so someone must presumably have done something about it. Like Herodotus in this if in nothing else, I tell only what I have been told; but four different and separate sources told me, so I am willing to believe.

The turning to the south at the Cyrene cross-roads leads to the main southern road, which runs from Barce to Ain Mara: a reasonably fast road, without the bends and steep climbs of the northern one, but without its interest too. The only place worth visiting is Slonta, where in the 1880s the Italian traveller Haimann discovered some strange carvings among the rock dwellings in the hillside. These lie about a hundred yards up the slope above the village of Slonta (dominated, like so many other villages in Cyrenaica, by its ruined Italian fort). In an overhanging ledge of rock large crude heads – rather like the Romano-British ones from Corbridge – jostle with smaller friezes of intertwined male and female figures. One can make out a horse, a horse's head, a bull, and some obscurer figures too badly weathered to recognize; also traces of carved moulding which seem to be of a type one should associate with the Roman period. In one place the sculptor has carved a column base out of the solid rock floor – whether for use or not one can't tell, but the whole column might have formed the strut of a timber, stone, or even a tiled roof. Almost the entire rock surface has been put to use with these carvings, yet there is no real sense of an overall composition: it is in some ways like an immense series of laborious doodles, a wall of three-dimensional *graffiti*. And who did them? A Libyan imitating Greek work at Cyrene? Or are they much earlier, with perhaps a few small details, such as the egg-and-dart mouldings, added later? No one knows, though the battered Antiquities Department sign down by the road, now almost illegible, ambiguously displays the two words 'Libyan Shrine'. I picked up several sherds of coarse Greek pottery on the slopes of the hill, and a few scraps of the black-glazed Attic ware; but they were sparse remains when compared with the quantities one finds on most Cyrenaican sites, and obviously the settlement at Slonta was a small one, perhaps entirely or almost entirely accommodated in the caves, and later in the tombs, most of which are still inhabited.

On one visit, a man who was playing cards in a group outside a house by the road willingly let us photograph not only the carvings but also the carved lintels of some uninhabited tombs now used for storing fodder, but when we tried to take a picture of an inhabited cave farther up the slope we were politely discouraged. And why not? Who would like a stranger peering over the hedge of 39 Acacia Avenue and taking a snap of the strange English at food? One's annoyance at the Libyan dislike of the camera (so different from the cheerful attitude-strikers who ruin every shot one takes in Egypt) should be modified with a proper respect for the cause of the dislike, which has much more to do with simple instrusion than any Islamic notion of the sinfulness of images.

Back on the northern road, after twelve miles, one gets as quickly as possible through Beida, the new unitary capital of Libya and arguably the ugliest town in the kingdom. Government buildings and flats and houses for civil servants rise everywhere out of dust or mud, looking derelict before they are even finished. The giant dome of the Parliament Building is losing its gold-leaf, Barclays Bank is housed in what looks like a shanty, and the ornamental fountain put up to celebrate independence looks like something bought up cheap after the 1951 Festival of Britain – an incongruous multi-coloured piece of post-war frivolity that sorts oddly with the bright blancmange pink of the Islamic University which stands on the other side of the road. This, centred on Beida because of its association with Mohamed Ben Ali Senussi, the founder of the Senussi movement and the grandfater of King Idris, is much envied by the University of Libya, not on any spiritual or scholarly grounds but because its budget is extravagantly larger, so that students' grants, for example, are far ampler than those given to our students in Benghazi and Tripoli.

There is no water in Beida itself, so water is specially piped from Ain Dabbusia in a valley about twelve miles away. The supply is poor, and one comes across stories of civil servants shaving in Ben Gascir mineral water, or even beer – itself a difficult liquid to come across in the heart of 'dry' Cyrenaica, and normally only available at the huge Beida Palace Hotel, which is always full of disgruntled Tripolitanian politicians and frustrated foreign diplomats staying in Beida while they waste their time waiting for some minister or other to come back from Tripoli or Benghazi. The supply of local labour to do the cooking, cleaning, butlering, and all the other ancillary tasks that go with government, is small and untrained. The climate is, if anything, even colder than Cyrene's, and though Beida had an existence in ancient times (as the town of Balagrae), there are few signs of it within the modern town boundary; and there are few scenic diversions, unless one counts the sight of the Crown Prince, Hasan el Rida, being whisked down the appalling main street in his Mercedes, flanked by a posse of sinister-looking motor-cycle outriders. Nowadays the Crown Prince, rather than the King, performs such ceremonial tasks as the opening of Parliament at Beida, as public grooming for the day when he will succeed to the throne.

It is a relief to get out of the expensive and useless squalor of Beida into the cedars and vineyards of the area round Messa, where the grapes for Cyrenaica's Giannaclis wines are grown. These fertile and well-organized acres were, together with the wheatfields of the Barce plain, the most intensively developed by the Italians in the whole of Cyrenaica. Some substantial remnants of this still survive, not only in the profitable fields themselves but also in the great Italian mansion which is now one of the

King's many palaces (though he seldom stays there) and in the hospital at Messa, which is still run by Italian nuns – a surprising relic in Cyrenaica, which elsewhere threw out most vestiges of Italy and the Italians, good and bad.

A turning north at Messa leads eventually to El Haniya, fourteen miles away on the coast. The road, which was bad enough to begin with on our early visits there, quickly deteriorated when the road-contractors got to work and two of the grimmest drives I made in Libya were attempts to get to or from El Haniya while the contractors' efforts were still dragging on, through the baking hot summer of 1966 and the unusually wet winter of 1966–7. The first was the steep ascent out of the village (for in rapid succession one has to negotiate the two steps of the Jebel, which along this stretch of the coast are close together), when the road was inches deep in red dust, difficult for the tyres to find purchase, and so volatile that the strain of driving quickly in low gear threw up clouds of dust in such quantities that the whole of the inside of the van was thick enough for Lucy (then aged four) to be invisible in the back seat: all I could hear were her alarmed screams as I grimly swerved and ground on up the unseeable road. When we got to the top at last, we found that our faces, our clothes, and the whole inside of the vehicle were thickly coated with vermilion dust. The other drive was shorter, because we actually got stuck in a January quagmire, just as the sunlight was fading. By the time I realized that the road was impassable, it was too late: in attempting to turn round, the tyres had jammed deep in the thick, red, glutinous mud. All the old desert routine of digging under the wheels and shoving in flat stones and sacks was useless, though we tried for three hours: the tyres had become so viscous that they spun and slithered whatever we did. At last a Land-Rover appeared through the darkness on its way down to El Haniya: only a Land-Rover should have attempted such a surface. The driver told us that he would come back soon with a tow-rope, though as the minutes dragged on I took it that this was just a kindly response to make us feel better. But eventually back he came, with a length of thick plaited wire which he attached to both bumpers, and at last, with much banging and crashing, we were pulled free, and got back on the firm road again. The whole episode gave me some idea of what conditions must have been like in the winter of 1941–42, when the rains were heavy and army vehicles bogged down all over Cyrenaica.

Such help is one of the most cheerful and attractive things about living in Libya. Whenever one breaks down, there is always someone who appears out of somewhere or nowhere and offers help: this is true Bedouin hospitality, the courtesy of the desert, and among all the narrowness and cramping of the country (to Western sensibilities) this must be counted strongly and affirmatively in any assessment. I remember, for example, the day in the low road of the Wadi Kuf, when I had a flat tyre and discovered – since it was the first flat tyre I had ever had in the van – that the tool thoughtfully provided by the manufacturers wouldn't dislodge the nuts on the wheel. The driver of a heavy lorry stopped, raked out from his cab a spanner that looked more like something to do with a locomotive, took off the wheel, put on a new one, and then presented me with the spanner, despite my protestations. And this was only the first of several such times, without which we would have been stranded and helpless.

From a distance, El Haniya looks like a noble citadel, perched on the steep cone of a hill; but as you get closer you see that this is simply a devastated shell, yet another superficially imposing Italian ruin, this time bombarded from the sea as well as from the air during the war. What remains of the village is huddled round its base, and there is little of it. But if you drive through the narrow gap by the police station, where the surfaced road ends, you come on to a rough track which skirts the edge of the *sebkha* and runs parallel with the sea. Another track soon leads off to the right, towards a low prefabricated bungalow which is the King's bathing hut – no longer used, like almost all the King's establishments, still patrolled by vigilant men of the Cyrenaican Defence Force. Keeping on the original track, which eventually leads to the mouth of the Wadi Kuf, you soon reach a wide bay of white sand, and with careful judgement you can get within a couple of hundred yards of the sea without getting bogged down. This was one of our favourite places in Libya. In summer, the whole plain towards the Jebel is a golden mass of waving barley: in front is nothing but sand, rocks, and sea. A small white *marabout* (Sidi Rahman) glitters to the south, and down on the coast is a whole complex of rock-cut pools and channels where the children could play and paddle safely. Offshore is a low island, with splendid underwater swimming. Even more attractive to me was the steep mound to the east, which was the explanation – if only a partial or inexplicable one – of these pools and channels.

For here I soon discovered that there lay, between the bay and the King's beach-house, a whole rich area of early settlement which, though cursorily touched on, had never been at all adequately explored. It does not even appear on the definitive *Tabula Imperii Romani*,* though clearly it was occupied well into Roman times and beyond. For over a hundred yards, these low cliffs west of the beach-house are thick with pottery: black-glazed Greek at the bottom, Byzantine at the top, and all types of Hellenistic and Roman in between. On the edge of the sea are man-made pools, steps, pits and channels, all cut in the solid rock. These can be found, too, on the seaward side of the island in the bay, which has the levelled and weathered remains of what looks to have been a lighthouse. All along the mainland cliffs are traces of foundations and much dressed stone. On one visit a friend found a Corinthian capital, made of local limestone, buried under the sand; and such an elegant piece of work – the foliage scrolls elaborately contrived so that the whole stone seemed to move – argues that El Haniya must have been something more than a tiny fishing port. On the Society of Antiquaries map, it lies unmarked between Ausigda (Ain Jarjarumma) to the west and Phycus (Zaviet el-Hamama) to the east, both of them less impressive sites than El Haniya. But I was hampered because the cliffs run down to the King's beach-house, and once or twice a Cydef man emerged from his palm-fronded sentry-box to warn me off. Perhaps it's for this reason that the Department of Antiquities knew nothing about El Haniya except that it was 'a possible site'; and with the amount of work still to be done elsewhere in Cyrenaica, El Haniya may properly be a low priority. But I feel proprietary about the place, as I do about the settlement I found fifteen years earlier near Kassala.

For camping at El Haniya, we relied on bread and water from the village, unless we had full water-containers; the bread often arrived stale from Messa, since there was no bakery nearer, and the water was dubious. On one early visit I came to the open well

* *Map of Roman Libya, East Sheet – Cyrenaica:* compiled by Richard Goodchild. Society of Antiquaries of London, 1954.

when a man from the *mudir's* house was lowering an old olive-oil tin down the shaft. As the tin slopped back up again, I queasily noticed beetles and larvae sculling about in it, and when I asked the man whether it was drinking water – since I wanted to fill my containers – he roared with laughter; not, I think, primarily at the ludicrousness of the question, but at my pronunciation of *sherrub* (drinking); after all, *he* was going to drink, had probably been drinking it for years, and here was an ignorant *ferangi* who neither recognized good water nor could speak proper Arabic.

On the other side of Messa, towards Barce, another turning goes off to the right which leads to Targunia, a small settlement with a mosque and *zawia* and a few half-ruined Italian farmhouses. All along here there are rock-cut tombs, sacrcophagi, and the substantial ruin of a Greek farm, with a high eastern wall and two vaulted roofs, one still standing, the other collapsed among a wilderness of broom and nettles. The heavy rains in early 1967 made the Jebel greener and denser with vegetation than ever, and I had to hack my way through nettles chest-high to reach some of the tombs. The most impressive group is round an open 'court', three sides of it taken up with chambers cut into the face of the outcrop and free-standing sarcophagi, most with their humped stone lids smashed or with a small hole broken in the side – a sign of early tomb robbers – but a few look untouched. I found in the thick weeds a carved stone which looked as if it might have been a small altar-like embellishment originally attached by the back to the rock-face.

Near the vaulted ruin I came across an old man hacking out roots with a blunt sickle. After I'd greeted him and told him what I was doing (my camera made up for a lot of vocabulary), I noticed that he had cut his hand with his sickle and blood was pouring down his fingers; so I got cotton wool, disinfectant and a bandage from the van and dressed the cut for him. He looked about seventy, with eyes more grey-blue than brown, grizzled white beard and hair, and a fresh pink complexion – more like some northern peasant than an Arab. He said he was a poor man, no money, no food. Having little money on me, and no food, I gave him some cigarettes, but it was almost impossible to find out much about the place from him: he said there were many tombs around, but couldn't indicate any more than the ones we could see from where we were sitting. It turned out that he lived in one particularly elaborate tomb just across the road, with one chamber used as a storage place for fodder and wood, the whole surrounded with a brushwood fence. When I left, he offered up copious praises to God, and then bent back to his root-grubbing, trying to clear enough ground to grow a small patch of barley. TCP and Band-Aid seemed to exist in another world.

A wadi running down towards the plain here has the finest natural echo I've ever come across. We discovered it by chance one New Year's Day, a deliciously bright and green morning in spring – for there are such days even in January – when every leaf was sparkling and the sea in the distance was a hard, clear line of blue. We suddenly noticed, talking among ourselves, that a faint echo was coming back to us from the opposite hillside, and when we raised our voices, or shouted, or sang, a perfect one rang back. Perhaps it was something to do with the clearness of the air that morning, and not some constant virtue of the place itself, because on a later visit we walked down the wadi in one of the thick mists that occasionally come down in this part of the Jebel, reducing visibility to about ten yards, and found that the echo was not as we'd remembered it: the atmosphere was more like Scotland or Wales than north Africa, as it was another time when the failing light and dense, milky mist forced us to stop and camp for the night in an open space by a Muslim cemetery on the Targunia road. We imagined strange sounds and creakings from the cemetery, but in the morning there was no sign of anything that could have caused them – certainly nothing like the talkative yews of an English graveyard.

After the turning to Targunia, the main road begins its steep descent into the Wadi Kuf. Strictly, the lower and longer reaches of this whole complex of valleys is called Jarjarumma, the Wadi Kuf being the deepest of these, but most people use the one name to represent all. Wadi Kuf means 'valley of the caves', and since *kuf* and *cave* seem to have some affinity I tried to find out from the Professor of Arabic what the etymology of the Arabic word was; but I need not have asked, for the dogmatic reply was that 'The English got their word from Arabic'. It was useless to point out that cave came via Old French from Latin, and that *kuf* was more likely to have been picked up from the Romans by the caveless nomads of the Arabian peninsula: patriotic chauvinism had to score its point. One of the things that bedevils the Arabic language is that it is taken to be a gift of God, and therefore to delve into its pre-Koranic sources smells of impiety. This is no excuse for my lack of command of the language, but it helps to make the burden of my ignorance easier to bear.

At any rate, etymology apart, this deeply seamed area of sheer cliffs, deep caves, stony crags and thickly wooded hillsides is the most dramatic in Cyrenaica. Over the deepest part of the wadi, the main road runs across two Bailey bridges, built by the Royal Engineers as temporary structures in 1943 after the Italians had blown up the concrete ones on their retreat west. These have been renovated over the years, but their wooden planking still makes an alarming thunder-roll as vehicles go over them, and now an Italian firm has won the government tender to provide a new bridge. Heavy vehicles are supposed to use the low road, a largely un-surfaced one which for most of its course runs parallel with the wadi; since our Volkswagen, even unloaded, weighed a ton – and because anyway we enjoyed the ride – we often took this road in preference to the main one, and found a favourite camping place in a meadow (for once an English topographical term sounds right) by the side of the wadi. Here, on level grassy ground right up against the hillside, the children – true urbanizers – spent most of their time making 'houses' among the rocks above us.

Not far away, in a deep cave with a low overhang of rock, we found porcupine quills on the dusty floor, and pale yellow stalagmites and stalactites. This is Hagfet ed-Dabba (the Cave of the Hyena), one of the classic prehistoric sites of north Africa, and fully described by McBurney in his two books.* The ascent to the cave is just difficult and hazardous enough to be exciting to children, involving careful choosing of footholds and hand-grips in some places where the rock face is vertical for stretches of twelve or fifteen feet. The tangle of undergrowth harbours lizards, tortoises, and snakes, and we found one long thin whipsnake (the commonest non-poisonous variety) coiled round a long branch as we scrambled up. Unlike Hagfet er-Rejma, near Benina, the ground is so thick with vegetation that we never found any

* *The Stone Age of Northern Africa*, Penguin Books, and *Prehistory and Pleistocene Geology in Cyrenaican Libya*, Cambridge University Press.

flints, and in the cave itself McBurney had to dig a good way down before finding anything. Looking out from the high cave mouth over the tumbled rocks and flotsam of trees in the wadi bed, we felt like Palaeolithic man regarding his wild and intractable domain.

In the Wadi Kuf cicadas, crickets, rock-doves, and bats alternate their whirrings and whistlings and cooings as the day moves into night. One dark evening, as we lay on a rug in our grassy place and read by the light of a torch, a tiny shrew moved into the beam and sat quite still until I ambitiously tried to turn the full light on it, when it scuttled away. It can be cold down here, even in the height of summer, and the dew is very heavy; we found our sleeping-bags covered with damp when we woke in the morning, and the sun takes a long time to appear over the tops of the hills. Very little from the outside, or upper world, disturbs the low wadi: perhaps half a dozen heavy lorries each day, because the police regulations about the use of the Bailey bridges don't seem to be seriously applied, and occasionally some charcoal burners, who are more often heard than seen as they lop wood on the hillside.

Back on the main road, which the low road joins just beyond the end of one Bailey bridge and a police post, you move on up the valley between high caves and precarious boulders to a point where an English castle suddenly seems to have been deposited on an eminence to your right. This is Gasr Bu Nigdem, a defensive fort of the late Roman period, put up after the Austuriani began their incursions into the Jebel, one of a whole series of forts in and around the upper stretches of the Wadi Kuf. Though it is the best-preserved of the easily reachable forts (a surfaced road to the right leads to it after about half a mile), the most splendid of all Cyrenaican *gsur* can be reached more roughly but quite straightforwardly by turning left rather than right at precisely this point, six miles along a track which varies between cattle-rut and loosely packed stones – punishing for a vehicle but not dangerous, and worth the bumps, grinds, and strain on springs and stomach. Here, on a prominent hill, with fine views in all directions, is Gasr esc-Sciahden, which seems to translate into 'the castle of the two martyrs': an evocative name but an inexplicable one, since the Arabs would hardly have been likely to commemorate in this way a pair of Christian martyrs of, say, the Byzantine period. The vaulted ground and first floors are still there complete, their massive keystones and arches still firm and looking likely to endure for another fifteen centuries.

There seem to be three periods represented at Gasr esc-Sciahden: a central tower of the first century A.D., further fortified walls in the third century, and finally a bonding together of the two separate walls in the time of Justinian, making a single solid wall over six feet thick. All around are large cisterns, some of them cut deep into the rock, and two of them vaulted, though one has collapsed like a great broken snake into the nettles: both are very like the long vaulted cistern at Safsaf, near the Cyrene cross-roads. Goodchild thinks that the changes in the sixth century may have involved converting the place into a fortified monastery, and here one's mind runs on the 'two martyrs' name, though without evidence. Whatever the explanation, the whole complex of cisterns and living quarters, together with the very size of the main building as it towers up over forty feet above the high hill on which it's set, seem to point to the fact that it was intended to support a large community.

Now, there isn't a sign of habitation within sight, unless one climbs to the top of the roof and looks over towards Gasr Bu Nigdem, the tip of which can be seen in the distance, and to the right of it the white mosque of Messa. I have seen goats herded by women in bright blue *barracans* on the sloping ground below, and once we were approached by a man who told us that he was a Cydef corporal and lived near by: he was out of uniform and was carting his little boy about on his shoulders, but his geniality was spoiled for us by one of those stupid and unthinking actions which could just as easily have happened in England. A baby gecko ran on to the path in front of us, and when I called the children over to see it the Cydef man came too: as soon as he saw what it was, he shot out his foot and ground the little thing into the dirt. When he saw the effect this had (screams and tears), he blustered that it might have harmed the children: the excuse of many a grass snake-killing gardener in the suburban Home Counties, but it came unconvincingly from a countryman. Probably he was just trying to entertain us, and I felt miserable when he later came down to the car and started to apologize to everyone. There are as mixed feelings about taking life among Muslims as there are among Christians, and I wasn't in a position to lecture him on R.S.P.C.A. humanitarianism.

One further *gasr* is notable, back on the main road a little farther on, near Zawia Gasrtain, not so much because of what stands there today but because of the extraordinary thing found there. In the floor of a Byzantine church at Gasr Lebia, a labourer digging for building stones uncovered part of a vast mosaic, which the Department of Antiquities gradually laid completely bare and then removed to Cyrene for restoration, where it still remains. This mosaic – the finest ever found in Libya, even surpassing the one from the Basilica of Justinian at Sabratha – is made up of fifty panels, and like the Sabratha one is of Justinian's reign. It seems that the small town was called Olbia, but that for some reason it was greatly enlarged and embellished in the sixth century and was renamed Theodora, in honour of Justinian's empress. Why such a place, of no obvious importance, was picked out in this way is difficult to understand, though Justinian certainly initiated a considerable building programme throughout Cyrenaica; and it is surprising that Procopius, who everywhere in his *Buildings* seems inclusive and thorough, should have omitted such a wonder as this mosaic.

The fifty panels centre on one which records that the whole work was laid 'in the third year of an Indiction by Bishop Makarios', and this has been established as A.D. 539. Out from this run the other forty-nine squares, all of them linked by a continuous band of interlocking loops and plant forms. There are allegorical and mythological figures – a woman holding a wreath and a scroll, Geon the river god with a big amphora, the river gods Tigris and Euphrates, and Ananeosis, the personification of renewal, who is a jewel-hung woman looking out of a canopy which resembles a box at the theatre; birds, animals, and fish, including a peacock, bulls, horses, deer, ostriches, a lion, a bear, a leopard, and an eagle tearing the guts out of a calf; there are horsemen and satyrs, amphibious monsters and a merman, castles and towers, and a representation of the Pharos of Alexandria, foreshortened to show the bronze statue of Helios. The variety and ingenuity are staggering, and it seems in no way the product of a provincial or limited society. There is a full range of colours, and in many cases the Cyrene restorers have found little to do, for the tesserae both in setting and colour have stayed firm and bright.

The discovery of the Gasr Lebia mosaic caused a local furore that spread beyond the tiny modern settlement, which clusters round a less ruinous Byzantine church, adapted by the Italians as a fort and later converted into a school and medical centre for the area. There was a strong feeling among the inhabitants that the mosaic should be left where it was after clearing and restoration was complete, for there was a justifiable notion that such a treasure would bring tourists – and therefore money – into the place. At first the Department of Antiquities got its way, however, and section by section the panels were lifted and taken to Cyrene. But over the years a powerful lobby managed to persuade the Prime Minister that the original site was the right place, and now there are plans – long delayed, and likely to be many years in coming to completion – to move the whole mosaic back, along with the sections of the church's main nave which were dismantled, with a modern building housing and protecting both church and mosaic. As it is, one needs to get the permission of the Controller of the Department of Antiquities before one can get into the old vehicle workshop at Cyrene where the panels are ranged one by one all round the walls; though the Department of Tourism still blithely dishes out to all visitors to its Benghazi office an attractively produced pamphlet which urges tourists: 'The main nave of the Church and other two rooms all with mosaic floor are now fully uncovered, walled and roofed, open to visitors and tourists. Do not miss this unique opportunity to visit one of the finest and most interesting masterpieces of art.' It would be interesting to know how many 'visitors and tourists' have thereby travelled the ninety-five miles from Benghazi to Gasr Lebia, only to find that what they are seeking is forty-five miles farther on, and difficult to gain access to even when one gets there.

After Gasr Lebia the road back to Benghazi runs through country which gradually becomes less hilly, opening out into broader valleys with their ex-Italian farms, among which Bayyada stands out as a sad imitation of an Italian hill-top village: noble from a distance, it is only when one gets close that the shattered roofs and broken windows can be seen, the church boarded up and the real centre of life transferred to a row of wooden shacks on the other side of the road, the mean shops of modern Cyrenaica. So the way drops down to the Barce plain, leaving the high Jebel with its thick woods, deep wadis, hills and rocks: splendid guerrilla country where Omar Mukhtar was captured near Gasr esc-Sciahden, and where the Bedouin tents merge into the natural camouflage of tree, bush, and stone – so different from the arid plains and deserts, where the tents loom up in the distance from far off, isolated pockets of life in a great nothing. In the Jebel they seem self-effacing, the very opposite of the hill-top *gsur*, those assertive buildings of a people determined in their policy to pacify the country, just as 1,800 years later the Italians attempted, failing in a far shorter time and far more ignominiously. This highest and holiest region of Libya, so much the most obvious and immediate in its natural beauty and grandeur, is in some ways and in some moods the saddest of all; for here was the greatest city of the Pentapolis, with all that went to make it great; and now it is an acreage of ruins, its environs a picturesque wilderness, and its ransacked tombs shelters for straw and animals, and for nomads who have stopped wandering.

It was on the plain below Cyrene, on a drizzling early morning in April, with lowering grey clouds and a bitterly cold wind, that I saw a procession of men carrying a coffin down the steep slope below the ruins of theatres and temples, chanting slowly and heavily as they went. Someone who had lived in the tombs had died, and was on his way to the new cemetery by the new hospital: a procession which seemed an image not only of the high Jebel but of Libya itself.

8 Synesius of Cyrene

FOR most of its 1,200-odd years of existence, the Cyrenaican Pentapolis was thoroughly provincial. It lay on the periphery of Greek settlement. In the period when Athens was dominant on the mainland, it had little contact with Athenian culture; and later, when Alexandria replaced Athens as the intellectual capital of the world, it was Alexandria that drew off the cream of Pentapolitan talent, without giving much back in return. Of those men who are known to have been Cyreneans, all but one of the famous left and made their names elsewhere: Aristippus, the hedonistic philosopher who became Socrates's companion in Athens and who founded the so-called 'Cyrenaic' school which later contributed to Epicurean thought; Callimachus the poet, who worked as a cataloguer in the great Library at Alexandria; Eratosthenes, the mathematician and astronomer, who accurately calculated the circumference of the earth and who became head of the Alexandrian Library; Carneades, who founded the New Academy at Athens; and there is the shadowy figure of Simon of Cyrene, unknown except for his brief dramatic appearance in three of the four Gospels, when he carried Christ's cross on the road to Golgotha. All these were expatriates from their birthplace, a country which in its remoteness, its agricultural wealth, its emptiness and its philistinism must have been much like Australia in a more recent period: a place from which talented men left to win their recognition abroad.

The one exception is Synesius, poet, essayist, priest, letter-writer. At the time of his birth, somewhere between A.D. 360 and 370, Cyrene had been a Greek city for almost exactly a thousand years. From his letters, of which one hundred and sixty exist, we can judge that he was born there, or close by, for in one of them, addressing his brother, he writes of 'our motherland Cyrene'. He also writes of his descent from Eurysthenes, who led the Dorians into Greece, and claims that his ancestors arrived in Libya with Battus – much as some Americans show pride in saying that their forebears came over with the *Mayflower*. In the fourth century

A.D. Cyrene was still very much a Greek city, less important administratively than Ptolemais but nevertheless the most distinguished by tradition of the cities of the Pentapolis. This – the Hellenized sector of North Africa, as opposed to the Latinized part (which stretched from Morocco to 'Marble Arch') – was also a part of the Roman empire, originally a joint-province with Crete and administered remotely from Rome, more recently a unit on its own under the Emperor of the East in Constantinople. Synesius was deeply aware of his Greek inheritance, not only in his pride of ancestry but also in the fact that Greek was his language, as it was of all Pentapolitan city-dwellers. Yet he was proud of his Roman citizenship too: 'How dare they flaunt the Roman citizens,' he wrote in one of his letters,* when speaking of marauding Austuriani. In addition, he was perhaps the first man to refer to himself as a Libyan: in one letter he asks why he should be sad to see the degradation of Cyrene, and answers: 'Because I am a Libyan, because I was born here, and it is here that I see the honoured tombs of my ancestors.'

Nothing is known of Synesius's parents, though one can assume that they were comfortably established country landowners. He frequently speaks of his country estates south of Cyrene, though in fact no substantial villas, such as are found in Tripolitania at Dar Buk Ammera in Zliten, or near Tagiura, have yet been discovered in Cyrenaica: the 'fortified farm', commonly noted on the map with the Arab word *gasr*, was the typical centre of agricultural settlement in the eastern province. Whatever sort of building he lived in, at any rate Synesius seems to have inherited land, and from an early age he was destined by his family position to be a future leader of the community.

The first known event of importance in his life was his stay in Alexandria, beginning in about the year 394, when he studied under Hypatia, who became the strongest single intellectual influence on him. Alexandria at this time had no formal university as such, but rather was the centre of a number of conflicting schools and academies, each centring on a teacher who dispensed doctrine – Platonism, Aristoteleanism, Stoicism, Epicureanism, Christianity, and far stranger cults. The city was a great simmering

* Cf. *The letters of Synesius of Cyrene,* translated and edited by Augustine Fitzgerald, Oxford, 1926.

✳ 151

stew of paganism and Christianity, sects and heresies. Hypatia herself was a remarkable woman: the spirit of her teaching was truly Platonic and clear-headed, not muddied or curdled by the Neo-Platonic and Gnostic mysticisms that flourished in Alexandria. She was a mathematician, and taught geometry and astronomy as well as philosophy; and Synesius treats her in his letters as a rational, practical person, telling her how he is making an astrolabe, asking for materials with which to make a hydroscope. These characteristics of intellect and practicality combined with great personal beauty and serenity in Hypatia. She met a violent death in 415, not long after Synesius's own death, when she was torn apart by a mob of Alexandrian Christians who resented her teaching. She – and, incidentally, Synesius – are commemorated in Charles Kingsley's rather flowery and ample novel, *Hypatia*.

Athens, for so many centuries the source of new ideas and skills, had become stale and, even to Synesius, provincial; he visited it for a short time in 395, and was disillusioned. If Alexandria was the intellectual capital, Constantinople was the administrative one, for these were the early days of the Byzantine empire, with the old Roman dominions split between dual emperors. It is a mark of Synesius's importance to the community of the Pentapolis at an early age that in 397 he was appointed to lead an embassy to Arcadius, the Emperor of the East, in Constantinople. His brief was apparently to lay before Arcadius the problems of the Pentapolis and to ask for imperial help. There had been bad plagues of locusts; the Austuriani were increasing their raids on the fields and cities; and – a particularly delicate point – the military administration was corrupt. The normal practice was for non-Libyans to be appointed to the military governorship of the Pentapolis, and for foreign mercenaries to be drafted in as garrison troops. Synesius was dissatisfied with the governors: Cerealis, Gennadius, Anysius, Innocentius, Andronicus – almost all are branded in his letters as either shirkers or rogues. But at the time of his mission to Arcadius, what chiefly exercised Synesius was the inefficiency, and sometimes the downright cowardice, of the foreign troops; and he particularly mentioned the Thracians and the Marcomani (the latter a tribe from the borders of modern Germany, Poland and Czechoslovakia). At a later stage he had good words to say for the Dalmatians, but in his speech to Arcadius he pressed for a citizen-army of native Pentapolitans, a sort of Home Guard, to be properly equipped with weapons by the central authority.

Synesius's speech (or, it may be, public letter) to Arcadius carries the title *De Regno* – 'Concerning Kingship' – and it is a passionate plea to the Emperor to act boldly and resolutely to avert the collapse of the Pentapolis. Since Arcadius was a mere puppet in the hands of powerful court factions (under, in succession, a couple of praetorian prefects, a eunuch, a Goth, and his own wife, the Empress Eudoxia), it may seem to have been an empty academic exercise. Certainly it doesn't seem to have resulted in effective action. But within the succeeding five years Synesius was put in a position where his own actions were crucial.

This came with the offer to him of the Bishopric of Ptolemais. He was in many ways the obvious choice, and the initiative of his friend Theophilus, Archbishop of Alexandria, lay behind the offer. Synesius was a distinguished citizen, a skilled orator, an astute ambassador, a patriotic Pentapolitan; later – though presumably this could hardly have been judged at the time of the offer – he showed himself to be a military leader capable of organizing resistance. Yet he himself felt reluctant to accept, as one can see from the letter to his brother in which he set down his objections and difficulties. His least important objection was that he disliked the idea of giving up the gentlemanly pursuits of hunting, dogs and horses, the natural concomitants of a country landowner's life. It would not in fact have been necessary for him to abandon them, but he felt that they were not fitting for a priest in high position; and he was prepared to give them up if he accepted the call. Then there was the disruption of his family life. A priest should be celibate. Synesius was married (the marriage had been solemnized by the 'blessed hand' of Theophilus of Alexandria) and had children; he was not prepared to renounce them, nor was he prepared to remain married while pretending that he was not:

I therefore proclaim to all and call them to witness once for all that I will not be separated from her, nor shall I associate with her surreptitiously like an adulterer; for of these two acts, the

✳ 153

one is impious, and the other is unlawful. I shall desire and pray to have many virtuous children. This is what I must inform the man upon whom depends my consecration.

Synesius's third objection was that his ideal of the philosophical life would be harmed; and here crucial difficulties arose. For it is doubtful whether he was a Christian at all, in a formal sense, and this despite the fact that about a third of the inhabitants of Cyrene at the time were Christians. Certainly he never speaks of his baptism, though adult baptism was the rule rather than the exception in the early Christian era, and one would have thought that somewhere in his philosophico-theological remarks he might have mentioned the fact if he had indeed been so received and accepted. But more important is the fact that all his letters up until the time of his acceptance of the bishopric reflect Platonic rather than Christian thought, and even after his acceptance there are far more quotations from and references to Plato than any part of the Bible; and when he does quote from the Bible, he does so more frequently and readily from the Old Testament (Genesis, Numbers, Samuel, Jeremiah, the Psalms) than from the New.

But it is difficult, on Synesius's own evidence, to call him a pagan, though he was frank about the Church's stumbling-blocks: 'If I am called to the priesthood, I declare before God and man that I refuse to preach dogmas in which I do not believe.' These were tough words in the context of Christian North Africa, which not very long before had been bloodily involved in feuds and savagery between the orthodox and a wild succession of Arian, Donatist, and other heretics. 'For my own part,' wrote Synesius, 'I can never persuade myself that the soul is of more recent origin than the body.' There was also the unacceptability, to someone of Synesius's rational, non-apocalyptic, non-eschatological temper, of a total *Dies Irae*: 'Never would I admit that the world, with all its parts, must perish.' But the most stubborn difficulty lay at the root of all Christian doctrine, that of the resurrection of the body: 'As for the resurrection, such as common belief admits it, I see here an ineffable mystery and I am far from sharing the views of the vulgar crowd thereon.' 'The vulgar crowd' accepted a conventional paradise of milk and honey, white-robed perfection, angels and crowns and harps, a literal heaven beyond the stars.

No student of Plato, no disciple of Hypatia, could concur with such a coarse belief.

But Synesius capitulated:

If after those things have been made clear which I least desire to conceal, if the man who holds this power from Heaven [i.e. Theophilus] persists in putting me in the hierarchy of the bishops, I will submit to the inevitable, and I will accept the token as divine.

From that point until his death about eleven years later, he was episcopally responsible for a wide area of Cyrenaica. As spiritual leader of the Pentapolis, he inevitably clashed with the secular authority, especially with one particular military governor (or Dux), Andronicus. Andronicus was the son of a tunny-fisherman from Berenike, and despite lack of precedence, and what Synesius indeed regarded as the law, had managed to procure himself the post of Dux, probably – Synesius suggests – through bribery. Whatever Andronicus had been like at his job, it is possible that Synesius, with his faintly arrogant regard for his own breeding, would have resented the high office of such a plebeian:

Indeed, if nothing else, I am descended from those men whose lineage . . . has been engraved on the public monuments; whereas this fellow cannot tell the name of his own grand-father, nor even of his father, except by guess, and from a tunny fisher's perch on a crag he has come at a bound into the governor's chariot.

But Andronicus was to Synesius not just a jumped-up churl: he practised extortion, often by torture, and openly flouted Synesius's authority, to such an extent that in the end Synesius called for permission to excommunicate him; and this was granted. But in what Fitzgerald, in a note to his edition of the *Letters*, calls 'a curious epilogue to the struggle', Synesius later wrote to Theo-philus asking for the mercy of the church:

We have snatched him from the fell tribunal here, and have in other respects greatly mitigated his sufferings. If your sacred person judges that this man is worthy of any interest, I shall welcome this as a signal proof that God has not yet entirely abandoned him.

One might add that for Synesius to react in this way is in itself 'signal proof' not only that he was a merciful man but also a man with real power in the Pentapolis.

But Synesius found himself to be in effect a military leader as well as a spiritual one. In a letter to his brother, he writes impatiently of the uselessness of the 'official' troops, and goes on:

> I am dictating this letter almost from my horse. I myself enrolled companies and officers with the resources I had at my disposal. I am collecting a very considerable body at Asusamas* also, and I have given the Dioesta word to meet at Cleopatra. Once we are on the march, and when it is announced that a young army has collected round me, I hope that many more will join us of their own free will.

The enemy against which all this activity was aimed was the Austuriani, that inland tribe of native Libyans which two centuries earlier had threatened Leptis Magna: now they had spread across the Sirtica and swarmed up through the bleak pre-desert plains south of the Jebel Akhdar, carrying out quick destructive raids on the farms and sometimes even penetrating the towns for loot and for women and children, whom they carried off as slaves. Unfortunately Synesius didn't record their appearance, their customs, or their activities, apart from their raiding and their cruelty: probably he was never in a position to do so, since they struck so swiftly and then dashed back to their impenetrable wastes.

In other letters to his brother and to his friend Olympius, he writes of lances, scimitars, two-edged swords, and the need for good arrows. He says that he is constructing a machine 'that we may hurl long-distance missiles from the turrets, stones of really substantial weight' – clearly a type of *ballista*. And he writes a long and amusing letter to his brother about an engagement with the Austuriani, in which the forces from Balagrae (Beida) took part, when a boastful Pentapolitan (presumably by adoption) called Joannes the Phrygian, turned tail and fled: he 'galloped without reining up as far as Bombaea and he remained hidden in the cave there, like a field-mouse in its hole'. Incidentally, the loathing Synesius expresses at Joannes's long hair (more witheringly con-

---

* Possibly the modern Sousa, which at an earlier stage was called Sozusa, and before that Apollonia.

demned than even his boastfulness and cowardice) seems to under-line my supposition – based on the rather turgidly 'witty' essay he wrote called 'A Eulogy of Baldness' – that Synesius himself was bald at a relatively early age.

There were less dramatic duties, of course. In a long letter to Theophilus, probably written in 411, he asks advice about a tedious and undignified squabble between the priests of the vill-ages of Hydrax (Ain Mara) and Palaebisca (unidentified), which were formerly under the episcopacy of Erythrum (Latrun): the priests almost came to blows over the responsibility of a chapel lying between the two, each rushing in to set up a communion table without the knowledge of the other. In another letter of about the same period it is clear that Synesius sometimes travel-led on pastoral work into the southern extremities, perhaps as far south as Mekili, where there was certainly a settlement in the Byzantine period. Here he found inhabitants who had never seen the sea and who therefore refused to believe in the existence of fish: there are no perennial streams, and very few fish-bearing lakes or ponds, in Cyrenaica.

Elsewhere there are glimpses in the letters of activities which have little to do with either military or religious activities. There is a short and friendly one to Hesychius, the remains of whose house, with its dutifully religious and filial inscribed mosaics, can still be seen near the Agora in Cyrene. Synesius has trouble with a drunken slave, orders new clothes, and sends a Cyrenean horse to a friend in Greece with the recommendation that it has 'bigger bones but carries less waste flesh' than Greek horses – a pathetically wistful echo, perhaps, of his old activities as a country squire, more fully amplified in another letter, where he laments the fact that he has given away his dogs and his saddle and that his bow is sprouting mould. There are some lyrical pass-ages about the beauty of nature in the Jebel, not precise and topo-graphical enough, perhaps, to suit the modern traveller's eye, but one should not expect careful itemization from a philosophical Greek:

How delightful is the Zephyr wind as it stirs the branches gently; there are the varied notes of birds, the colours of the flowers, the shrubs of the meadow; here are the works of the husbandman, there nature's gifts. All things are fragrant with perfume, the aromas of a healthy soil. I will not praise the nymphs' grotto.* It would need a Theocritus. And there is something beyond all this.

There are references in the letters to ostrich hunting, for ostriches survived in Cyrenaica until the exterminations of the nineteenth century, and three mentions of silphium, already by Synesius's time evidently on the way to extinction, being cultivated in a small way in private gardens rather than being gathered commercially as a revenue-producing exported crop: earlier, this plant had been regarded as a panacea. And there is a good deal of philosophical discussion and speculation, often with an air of being a lofty mind stranded among philistines and peasants, which is one of Synesius's least endearing attitudes:

Since it interests you to know about my life, we study philosophy, my dear friend, and we have only splendid isolation for our fellow-worker, not one human being. I have never anywhere in Libya heard a man uttering a philosophical phrase except when an echo is repeating my own voice . . .

But gradually the concern with the depredations of the Austuriani grows more and more obsessive. He mounts guard in his cope, he spends his time patrolling between the watchtowers, he cannot sleep for the alarms: even the Dalmatians, the bravest of the foreign troops, cannot withstand the constant attacks:

They still patrol the heights, ever on the watch to drive back the attacks of the enemy, like whelps springing out from the courtyard, that no wild beast may attack the flock . . . Of what use are many levies and the annual cost of maintaining the troops here? For war we need hands, not a list of names.

Often in a month I have to rush to the ramparts, as if I received a stipend to take part in military service rather than to pray . . .

Alas! for the young men we have lost! Alas! for our crops which we hoped for in vain! We have planted our fields for the fires lit by our enemies. Our wealth for the most of us was our cattle, our herds of camels and of horses which grazed on the prairie. All are lost, all have been driven

* Apollo's shrine at Cyrene? The fountain at Gubba?

away . . . I write to you shut up behind ramparts and be-
sieged. Often in an hour I see torches gleaming, I am lighting
some myself, and raising them as signals to others . . . and I,
placed as a sentinel between two towers, am struggling
against sleep.

> To my lance I owe my bread,
> To my lance I owe my wine,
> Leaning on my lance I drink.

The most moving expression of these final years is the *Catastasis*, which has been given the date A.D. 412. It has been taken by
some commentators to be a private letter and by some to be a
speech. At any rate, its substance is a lament for the collapse of the
Pentapolis: 'Pentapolis is dead, extinguished; its end has come,
it has been assassinated, it has perished.' In it, Synesius foresees
his own death, which he takes to be a kind of martyrdom. Like
Eliot's Becket, there may have been an implicit desire for this,
and it is easy to take the final words as self-dramatizing. But, set
in the context of the place and the time, with Church and laity
alike embattled, they do not seem extravagant:

I shall remain in my place at the church. I shall place before me
the vessels of holy water. I shall cling fast to the sacred pillars
which hold up the inviolate communion table from the ground.
There will I sit while I live, and lie when I am dead. I am a
minister of God, and perchance I must complete my service
by offering up my life. God will not in any case overlook the
altar, bloodless, though stained by the blood of a priest.

It is not known, indeed, whether Synesius died at the hands of
the Austuriani, or how and when he died. The *Catastasis*, whatever
its date, seems an appropriate finale. In it, certainly, we find
the most eloquent and passionate epitaph for not only a way of
life that was quickly breaking down into anarchy (though Justinian, a century later, briefly revived the fortunes of the Pentapolis), but also for a man who preserved better than anything else
has done some notion of what that life was like. Synesius was,
after all, in effect right, despite Justinian: the Pentapolis was
finished, and, though he could not know it, Amr Ibn el-As, and
later the Beni Hilal and the Beni Suleim, were to wreak a destruction even more complete than that of the Austuriani, who were
themselves to be swallowed up in the astonishing Arab invasions.

The proud, lonely, aristocratic voice of Synesius was the last echo of Greece in North Africa, until, in a quite different form, the Muslim Cretans found refuge in Sousa in the late nineteenth century; and what they represented was hardly Greek at all.

I stumbled on Synesius almost accidentally, but for me he became an obsessive *persona*, through which, in however unhistorical and cavalier a way, I could express in my poems part of what Libya meant to me. Almost all the scholarly work on him has been theological or philosophical rather than historical, most of it by nineteenth-century German and French writers. Augustine Fitzgerald, a man of more literary tastes, could do little to establish Synesius as a creative writer in his two-volume edition of *The Essays and Hymns**: *De Regno* and *Catastasis* are powerful pieces of rhetoric, but their chief interest is not literary, and as for the homilies, the essays (such as *The Egyptian Tale* and *Concerning Dreams*) and the ten hymns, they seem to have small merit, at least through the medium of Fitzgerald's rather Wardour Street translation. It is only through the letters that one catches the tone of an individual voice.

It was Richard Goodchild's pamphlet on Cyrene and Apollonia that first led me to Synesius, and then some extracts from the letters included in the Chicago University volume on Ptolemais. I managed, through Goodchild, to borrow the Fitzgerald edition (long out of print) from the Antiquities Department at Cyrene, and even before I had finished reading it I began to see the shape and substance of my own 'Letters of Synesius', which use Synesius not so much as a consistent *persona* but as a running commentary, or chorus, on the conflicts, apprehensions, anomalies, strains, stresses and – in the Joycean sense – epiphanies I found in Libya and in myself. 'It seemed to me,' as Synesius wrote in one of his letters to Hypatia, 'that I was some other person, and that I was one listening to myself amongst others who were present . . .' It was not an antiquarian exercise but a compulsive extension of myself into something both alien and familiar. There might be an effect of historical *collage*, but the objects were always reversible – the past seen through the eyes of the present, and the present speaking with the voice of the past. The juxtapositions and voices are consistent within any one of my

* *The Essays and Hymns of Synesius of Cyrene*, Oxford, 1930.

twelve 'Letters', but the effect is meant to come from a total reading.

The flux and uncertainty of Libya in the early fifth century aren't, to be sure, the same as the flux and uncertainty of Libya today; but for me, somehow, Synesius united the two. Beyond that, my 'Letters' are not intended to have simply a Libyan relevance, needing an elaborate apparatus of footnotes: the change and decay on which they comment isn't purely local but is a multi-faceted process of cultural clash, the crisis of faith, and the heroism and puniness of individual comment. 'Modern', expatriate, rootless, liberal, Protestant, my sort of person in so many ways seems to be the very opposite of Synesius, with his pride, his intellectual snobbishness, his patriotism, his fine-drawn religious conscience. But many times, hearing the *muezzin's* stertorous cries ('In the Name of Allah, the Compassionate, the Merciful – Prayer is better than Sleep') echoing above the cosmopolitan babble and traffic of Benghazi, sounding uncannily like some Byzantine plainchant, I have imagined Synesius struggling with the mysteries which he was meant to interpret – the Trinity, the Eucharist – and knowing that beyond the lush paradise of the Jebel lay the miles of desert emptiness where the pagans plotted the future.

And throughout Libya I have glimpsed what Synesius saw as the inexorable process of gradual ruin: a Greek farm two thousand years old, an Italian colonial village of the 1930s, and a hut built of stone and mud only a few years ago – all subside and crumble and seem far less permanent than the Bedouin tents. As Evans-Pritchard puts it so well*:

> Time and again colonists, tempted from their homes by the short sea routes and the wooded plateau, have settled in the country and dispossessed the Bedouin, but in the end it is the Bedouin, and not the colonists, who have survived. When one looks at the massive Phoenician, Greek, Egyptian, and Roman ruins and the already half-ruined Italian towns, villages, and farms, and then on the flimsy tents of the Arabs, one cannot but reflect that the race is not always to the swift nor the battle to the strong.

Carved in marble or painted on a wall, a Greek inscription or a

* *The Sanusi of Cyrenaica,* p. 39, Oxford, 1949.

slogan of Mussolini's are equal emblems of time's corrosion. Yet the things of the past are not completely destroyed: they survive as their own witnesses. Within the same patch of featureless and stony Libyan ground you might pick up a Neolithic flint, a scrap of Greek pottery, a spent Italian cartridge, and an empty tin left by some oil-prospector who passed that way last year. In Libya you are made aware the whole time of the abandonment of things, the material leftovers of receding cultures.

It was Synesius who gave me the inspiration to embody and transmit that awareness; though I cannot imagine what he would make of the result, or what he would think of his responsibility for it. He had no false modesty about his place among his fellow human beings, certainly. When debating with his brother about the offer of the Ptolemais bishopric, and having reached a point when he knew his conscience must force him to accept, he wrote: 'A camel with the mange, says the proverb, can shoulder the burden of many asses.' That is one of Synesius's voices. I hope he will forgive me for having ventriloquized with some others.

9   Black Monday – before and after

ON Thursday, June 1st, 1967, the English staff of the University of Libya in Benghazi assembled at eight o'clock in the morning, dressed in an *ad hoc* uniform that could have been interpreted as having sinister implications: white shirts, black trousers, black ties, and black armbands. Each of us had a duplicated list of instructions, timing our movements down to the very minute. Quietly we took our places in a small convoy of vehicles, and waited.

There were in fact no implications more sinister than those normally associated with a funeral. We were the coffin-bearers in the funeral procession for our oldest colleague, Fred Koerner, an Englishman who had spent almost the whole of his working life teaching in the Arab world, first in Egypt (where he arrived the term after Robert Graves left), and then – after the riots and expulsions in Cairo – at the University of Libya from its foundation. What made this funeral a unique occasion was that this was the first time in the shortish history of the University that a member of staff, of any nationality, had died in office. This being so, our senior Libyan colleagues wanted to make the funeral a precedent for all later ones, an impressive and well-organized display of university mourning. A series of meetings had evolved a 'document of procedure' which was military in its explicitness and close timing.

After collecting the huge wreaths from the Botanical Gardens – wreaths from the Minister of Education, the Mayor of Benghazi, the university administration, the various faculties, the students, and so on – we fetched the coffin from the British Military Hospital and drove back, into the middle of town, where the cortège was to form up at 10.15. Here, under banners of black crêpe, a great procession of Libyans, Egyptians, and Englishmen started out on foot, slowly following a vehicle which was in fact a university furniture van, but so swathed with ribbon and crêpe and wreaths that it was almost, but not quite, unrecognizable. On it was Fred's coffin. We all moved down Istiklal, preceded by motor-cycle policemen, the street itself lined with policemen and men of the Cyrenaican Defence Force. It was an impressive business.

Five days later it seemed even more impressive (and unlikely) in retrospect, when Istiklal was a howling mass of students and others, rapidly moving from stoning the American Embassy to burning down the American Cultural Centre, and then on to burn the British Consulate, the British Council, the British Embassy reading-room, and some dozen or fifteen other carefully selected sites in Benghazi. The Dean of the Faculty of Commerce, who on June 1st had solemnly walked in line with his fellow Deans behind Fred Koerner's coffin, on June 5th was leaping about in the courtyard of the University, urging the students out into the streets with banners, shouting for burning and destruction. For that morning, June 5th, we had all heard that Israeli planes had attacked Cairo, and within a very short time the news had also spread that Britain and America were actively giving support to the Israeli effort. Whatever the truth or otherwise of this, no Englishman or American could feel anything but vulnerable.

Those first few days of June 1967, between Fred's funeral and the violence of burning, blur into one another with events that seem linked with irony. On June 3rd, there were the British celebrations for the Queen's official birthday, one of those expatriate events seemingly frozen in some pre-1914 era, with military counter-marching and the Consul-General wearing a strange hat while he takes the salute, and even stranger hats, worn by the women, at the party on the Residence lawn in the evening. Archaic but not offensively nationalistic, the whole affair seemed to be managed with appropriate discretion, at a time when the tension between the Arab states and Israel was building up, with the Gulf of Aqaba blocked and the United Nations force withdrawn from the Gaza strip. There were, in fact, few Libyan guests at the evening party, though many had been invited; but this, though disappointing, was not unusual, for most Libyans naturally find it embarrassing to stand about at a party where alcohol is consumed in what may appear to be gross quantities. It seemed charitable to suppose that they had stayed away for such non-political reasons.

Not that feelings in Libya about Israel ought to be minimized.

A few months after our arrival in 1965, posters suddenly appeared all over Benghazi, in Arabic and English: broken gothic type on lurid pink and yellow paper proclaimed such slogans as 'No world pease whill illeagal Isreil exists' and 'Palesting was not Belfors land to promise'. This was said to be the work of local members of the Palestine Liberation Front. As in almost all Arab countries, Israel did not officially exist. Censorship naturally followed from this attitude: all imported foreign newspapers were subjected to scrutiny, and any reference to Israel, however slight, was cut out. One morning, when I was standing in the Central Post Office to collect a parcel, I watched a man waiting while his consignment of imported pocket diaries was inspected by the customs officer, who went through each one, turning to the tiny atlas at the back and blacking out with his ball-point pen the state and the name of Israel. Globes on sale in the stationers were similarly treated.

We – the British teachers – were naturally discouraged by the British Council from so much as mentioning Israel to students and Arab colleagues; a few years earlier, an Englishman in Agedabia had rapidly been expelled from Libya for discussing, with supposed impartiality, the Palestine Problem. But I couldn't keep total silence. Discussing the concept of the scapegoat, as an aspect of the treatment of Snowball in *Animal Farm*, I one day ventured to a class that Hitler had used the Jews as scapegoats. 'And Hitler,' came a voice from the back of the class, 'was right.' There was a murmur of general agreement. To shake my head and suggest some bias on their part was a weak gesture; but it was as far as I got.

The day after the Queen's birthday party, June 4th, I drove down into the desert about a hundred miles south-east of Benghazi. I took some friends – Pablo Foster, who had been there before, was our guide – and together we were going to pick up the young British anthropologist who, as I mentioned in an earlier chapter, had been living with a Bedouin family: part of a scheme of linked research between Durham University and the University of Libya. As in most of the Libyan hinterland, there are no roads in this area, just camel and goat tracks, and sometimes not even that. Twice we missed our way, for there are no accurate maps and few landmarks to steer by; and both times we had to rely on help given by Bedouin who suddenly seemed to loom out of nowhere. The first time it was a very old blind man, all alone in a small tented encampment while the rest of the family was off getting in the barley. Although he couldn't see, he seemed to sniff the air before pointing us in the direction we ought to take. He didn't mislead us, but about half an hour later it was necessary to ask the way again, when two younger men appeared over a slight rise in the ground. One of them insisted on getting into the van and putting us on the right track; and when, about eight or ten miles farther on, he felt we couldn't go wrong, he got out. We offered to drive him back, but he wouldn't hear of it: he was quite prepared to walk those eight or ten miles in the heat of the day, expecting no reward, simply to get some strangers to their destination.

When we reached the encampment where the anthropologist had been staying, the warmth of the welcome was even stronger. The sheikh was a learned, dignified and imposing figure. Almost all Cyrenaican Bedouin are followers of the Senussiya, and therefore feel close to the King, the maker of those ties with Britain during the Second World War which still seemed to stand firm on June 4th. The sheikh's brother at one point put his two forefingers close together and said: '*Ingliz, Senussi, wahad-wahad*' – the two are one. I had heard the phrase before and had felt the force and sentiment behind it. Whose fault was it that the words seemed to ring hollow back in Benghazi the following day, June 5th, Black Monday?

But in between the desert expedition and the events of June 5th there was another occasion: on the Sunday evening a party was held at one of the American Embassy houses to say goodbye to the director of the American Cultural Centre and to welcome his successor. George Neifeh, the director who was going, was himself of Arab ancestry, and his wife was a colleague of mine at the university. Unlike the Queen's birthday party, there was a fair number of Libyan guests, including Doghman, who had just been elevated to Rector of the university after being Dean of the Arts Faculty. Despite the situation, or perhaps because of it, there was hardly any political talk. Doghman seemed to spend most of his time talking to me about Libyan folk-poetry. We stood about on the lawn – a rare treat in Benghazi – under the eucalyptus trees, in as relaxed and friendly a cosmopolitan atmosphere as I can remember in Libya. Within less than twenty-four hours, almost timed as a farewell gesture to the Neifehs and a welcome to their successors, the American Cultural Centre was in flames.

On the Monday morning I was in the examination control-room in the university, picking up one set of exam scripts and delivering another. At about 9.30, some of the Egyptians came in and said that Radio Cairo had just announced a heavy Israeli air raid on Cairo. My first reaction – and I voiced it quite spontaneously – was, 'The fools, the *fools* – this is the end of Israel.' The Egyptians weren't noisily demonstrative or jubilant. One of them said quietly, 'Our whole history has led up to this point.' There was no talk at that moment of British and American involvement, though the propaganda barrage from Radio Cairo must already have begun. As the word spread of what had happened, one of the Englishmen dashed back to his place to get a radio capable of getting the B.B.C. World Service on shortwave: otherwise one would have to wait for the Forces Broadcasting relay of it, which wouldn't come through until the evening. But for those first several hours, someone was doing some effective jamming, and we could hear nothing at all from the B.B.C. Radio Cairo was playing almost continuous martial music and soldiers' choruses, interspersed with loud patriotic exhortations. Radio Libya seemed to have the music without the exhortations.

But it wasn't until Doghman and Orebi, the two senior university men on the spot, put up a notice postponing indefinitely all examinations, and the students ran out into the streets and squares with banners (some rapidly done on the spot, others apparently prepared beforehand), that I began to realize pretty sharply that what was going on wasn't simply a matter of a war several hundred miles to the east, with which Libya, an Arab state, would naturally feel involved: the mood of the students was that Libya *was* involved, that there was war here too.

Already our children had been sent back from school, and indeed the first my wife knew of the war was their knocking at the door to announce their return three hours earlier than usual: the school had been closed as a precaution by the British Embassy. With nothing to do at the university, I thought – abstractedly, it now seems, though it made sense at the time – that I might as well go to arrange for the packers to come and crate our belongings, for we were due to leave anyway in early July. Danger hadn't occurred to me: nobody had set fire to anything yet, and although there were a lot of people in the streets and some rather aimless shouting now and then, there was nothing one could call a mob at work. It was as I was driving towards the packers along one of the main carriageways in Benghazi that I saw the first sign of what was to come. I was waved down by the police to pull up by the side of the road, to let through a horde of lorries and cars coming in the opposite direction into the town: every vehicle swarming with demonstrators shouting and waving flags and banners. Above the bonnet of the leading lorry one man was waving the flag of the U.A.R., while next to him another man held up a huge framed portrait of Nasser. In the following lorry, a third man waved the green black and red flag of Libya – and next to him, a fourth elevated, for all to see, a frame as big as Nasser's. But it was empty. It held no picture. Everyone knew the significance of that: where was Idris, what was he doing, when was he going to give the word?

The cavalcade surged on, taking no notice of me, except for one man who shouted out 'Fucking Americans and British' in a rather nice voice. At the packers, business seemed as usual, and I fixed a date three weeks away for them to come and deal with our stuff. It wasn't until I was driving back into Benghazi that I realized real trouble had begun. As I passed the end of the road between the university administrative buildings and the American Embassy, I caught a sudden glimpse of a large crowd hurling stones, and a water-sprinkler machine ineffectively trying to disperse the crowd by going straight down the middle of the road. And as I turned the corner of Istiklal into 9th August Square, where our own block was, I saw that the American Cultural Centre was in flames up to the second floor.

I parked the car as inconspicuously as possible on the far side of the square, but I felt that our big white van was so well known in Benghazi as a foreigner's vehicle that it was apt to be attacked wherever I put it. I also walked as inconspicuously as possible, keeping well behind the crowd, and then covered the last thirty

yards down Sharia Misurata to our block in a sprint – only to find
when I got to the entrance that the big heavy door had been firmly
shut, obviously so as to prevent the mob getting in. I beat on it
in what I'm sure was a panicky way, calling on the *ghaffir* Saad
to let me in, which he did, muttering '*Mush qwayyis*' to himself
and shivering. Upstairs, Ann and the children and Stephen Levinson were sitting in the living-room, playing, of all things, Happy
Families, with the shutters shut and the lights on. The tempera-
ture inside was ninety-seven degrees; but it seemed safest to have
the shutters pulled, if only to prevent the children from dashing
on to the balconies and attracting attention to themselves and our
flat. So we sat and tried to concentrate on Master Mouse and Mrs.
Mole, so that the children wouldn't be distressed by the shouting
and smell of burning outside. But from time to time we couldn't
stop ourselves jumping up and peering through the shutters, and
even at one point went up on the roof, where at least we couldn't
be seen by the crowd, and from which we had a good view over the
rising plumes of smoke which were beginning to be noticeable all
over Benghazi, especially between Istiklal and the sea (so that it
seemed apparent that the British Embassy as well as the American
had been fired), and towards the Souk, so that presumably the
Jewish shops were suffering and the synagogue too.

By now the local Forces Broadcasting Service was on the air,
relaying the B.B.C. World Service news bulletins every hour – a
series of extreme contradictory claims from the Arab forces and
the Israelis. The electricity failed, so that even in the brightness of
the early afternoon the flat was in semi-darkness. Outside, a helicopter droned over the town, a big explosion marked what later
turned out to be the dynamiting of Bedussa's shop in Istiklal, and
now and then there were bursts of what seemed to be machine-gun
fire. But after a time things became quieter, as people presumably
went home to have their afternoon sleep, so I decided to venture
out into the square to try to park the car closer to the flat: it was
so far unharmed, and I had the feeling we might be needing it.
One Cydef man stood outside the smoking ruins of the American
Cultural Centre, with helmet and fixed bayonet: at the time of the
firing, seven Cydef men who had seemed to be on duty outside the
building had quickly nipped round the side, a narrow street
between the Centre and the Misr Bank, where they had kept out

of sight until the mob had finished its work. But now the one man had nothing to do but loll sleepily in the shade, with the fragments of charred books and magazines stirring behind him.

The only other people in the square were a couple of university students, one of whom I recognized as one of my second-year men, an earnest but not notably bright chap. He walked across the square purposefully towards me, bent, I supposed, on saying something about the situation, and – who knows? – perhaps bemoaning the fate of the Cultural Centre, a popular place for students doing last-minute work for the exams, because of its nearness to the university, its comfortable chairs and its coolness. But after the usual greetings, it was apparent that only one thing concerned him: 'Please, sir, have you yet marked our Shakespeare examination?' Perhaps he was right: perhaps he had got his perspectives straighter than anyone else. But at that moment it seemed a question so ludicrous in its triviality that I didn't have the patience to give him a serious answer, but simply indicated the gutted building behind us, and left him to brood on what he had or had not done about *Julius Caesar*.

Early in the evening the British army families began to be evacuated from the town. A curfew had been imposed at 8 o'clock by the government, and soon after this an army lorry drew up outside the block of flats opposite, where a corporal in the Inniskillings lived with his wife and two young children. Within five minutes they had loaded their suitcases, and were off, to refuge in Wavell Barracks. It certainly didn't strike us that we ourselves should get, or needed, such treatment, but later in the evening B.F.B.S. began broadcasting every few minutes an announcement to all British and American civilians. We were told to have ready one suitcase per person, knife, fork, spoon, and two blankets: all other possessions were to be locked away as securely as possible and keys were to be labelled. At 1 o'clock on Tuesday morning, while we were sleepily packing all our other possessions into cardboard boxes, for a final shipment that now seemed unreally remote, the radio advised all civilians to listen to an important announcement at 0315. By now there seemed no point in going to bed. The announcement told us that two convoys of army lorries would leave from the centre of Benghazi, following two separate routes, and stopping at set points on the way: the timings were to be given later, and we were to join the appropriate convoy, with transport of our own if we had it, at those times.

At 4 o'clock the announcement of timings was given, and we had ten minutes to wake and dress all four children, bundle our suitcases together, and stumble down the unlit stairs towards the car parked outside. Saad, roused from his sleep in his little cupboard under the stairs, groaned and commiserated as we tripped over things and hurried out into the dark. To him and to us, it seemed the last time we should see him. None of us really imagined we would ever get back to the flat, for the whole direction of the army scheme seemed to be one of evacuation – first to the barracks, then planes back to England. The curious thing was that we felt so unmoved by the thought of losing almost everything: we thought we attached a good deal of importance to possessions, and the flat was full of books and antiquities and treasured junk, as well as clothes and toys and domestic things. Yet the apparent loss of all this hardly occurred to us. We were safe.

The drive out to the barracks in the early morning took us in a long column of cars and lorries, bumper to tail, past the wreckage of June 5th. Bedussa's was the most shocking sight. It was as if a bomb had fallen. The roof was blown off and the first floor collapsed and sagged into the rubble of his stock underneath. It was later, in the barracks, that we began to hear the more lurid stories about what had been going on, part of a conflict of rumour and confirmed fact that went on for days afterwards. The most bloody concerned the NAAFI club in town (the so-called 'Ace of Clubs') and the American Embassy. The NAAFI club was on the first floor of a block of shops, close to the Elizabeth Arden cosmetic shop, which was also fired, since it was managed by a Jew. The club was reached by a narrow staircase, up which the mob tried to force itself. Upstairs there were a handful of NAAFI girls, too terrified to leave the place, and an R.M.P. man who had been sent in to escort them out. As the crowd started up the stairs, the military policeman grabbed the nearest thing to hand – a fire extinguisher attached to the wall – and hurled it down the stairs, catching the first man full-tilt in the chest, so that he collapsed back against all those behind him. He was killed, one of the few casualties in Benghazi; unlike Tripoli, where the material damage was much smaller but where a dozen or so Jews were killed, some of them through being thrown from balconies and windows. Later, when the club was empty, the crowd returned and destroyed it.

The situation at the American Embassy was even worse. Here, after pelting the place with stones, smashing every window, some of the wilder men managed to get up on the roof and started breaking their way in through the skylights, paying no heed to the damage they were doing to themselves – slashed veins and arteries: the American consul said 'it was like a Jackson Pollock painting – blood splattered from wall to wall and ceiling to floor'. By this time, the Embassy staff had shut themselves in the downstairs vault, while they assembled the arsenal of weapons and tear-gas which might make it possible for them to get out. As they emerged, they tossed the tear-gas canisters at the crowd, but many were thrown back, though not before they had severely burned the hands of the attackers, for these canisters apparently grow white-hot as they are released, thus letting the gas escape. The Americans were pushed back into the vault, with such force that one Libyan, eagerly pressing forward to assault the consul, was caught in the jamb and had his head crushed (inevitably, in the words of the consul, 'like a rotten apple') in the heavy metal door. Eventually, a small force of British troops arrived and managed to extricate the Americans. Another British group, the six-man crew of a Saracen armoured car, were surrounded in their vehicle when it stalled on the waterfront near the British Embassy; some members of the crowd had petrol cans which they poured on to the vehicle and set alight, and as the crew struggled to get out they were dragged into the road and beaten. Most of them were severely burned, and one was flown out of the Embassy by helicopter.

In general it seems that, as one might expect, the crowds were led by men with some sense of organization and planning: whether they were 'Egyptian agents' (frequently and dogmatically said by British and Americans) or not is another matter. They had transport, they carried petrol, and they were methodical, though of course their followers weren't always so. For example, on the late afternoon of June 5th a colleague of mine who lived in a block of flats at the end of the dual carriageway, close to a timber-yard owned by Bedussa, saw a lorry arrive, along with a number of cars and motor-cycles, the occupants and drivers break into the yard, smash bottles of petrol over the piles of wood, turn over the owner's car, and set the whole place on fire. Most of them then left in a body, but he saw twenty or so hang about aimlessly, or as if looking for something else to do. They looked along the line of cars parked outside the block, appeared to be in some doubt about which were European or American-owned, and after rocking them a little they left.

In D'Aosta camp, the atmosphere was one of some great wartime operation, all achieved with considerable British phlegm and good humour. Accommodation was found for well over 1,500 civilians – including Americans, Germans, Dutch, and a sprinkling of others – in a camp designed to hold only 400 soldiers. The soldiers were with us as well, engaging in warlike exercises on the barrack square while we looked on. We slept in workshops and gymnasiums, sheds and hangars. For one night, until Ann and the children left, we were in the so-called French Room of the army school, and later I slept in something called the Games Cupboard. Much time was spent in queuing for food, beer, cigarettes, and the NAAFI-price goods which seemed absurdly cheap to us, civilians restricted to the inflated open market in Benghazi. In the first couple of days of that six-day incarceration there was a good deal of wild, rather hysterical drinking, which went with a feeling of irresponsibility: indeed, the drink stocks were rapidly exhausted and couldn't be replenished, as the liquor warehouses, owned by Jews in the town, had all been burnt out. Then a sense of order began to prevail. The civilians began to draft duty-rotas for themselves, to help with the cookhouse chores for example, and I spent long sweaty hours washing mounds of plates and mugs. A daily cyclostyled bulletin of camp news was distributed, telling us, among other things, how pleased the camp commandant was with 'the standard of cleanliness that has been attained'.

But there was a tension under everything, and people showed the strain in different ways: talking too much, not talking at all, wild outbursts at trivialities, some tears. On Tuesday evening it was announced that there was limited space on some of the Kingdom of Libya Airlines flights going via Tripoli to Rome, with priority given to mothers with a number of children. Ann and our four clearly qualified for this, and we managed to get them off on the Wednesday morning, with the few things we had been able to collect before we abandoned the flat early on Tuesday. But it was a long-drawn-out return to England. Benina Airport was full of Algerian MiG fighters *en route* to the war, and all flights were delayed there. Then in Tripoli there was an alarming three-hour wait while the airline officials argued with customs men and armed forces, the latter apparently eager to commandeer the planes, which they said – in a sense correctly – were government property and therefore should be used for the war effort, not by alien civilians fleeing the country. All this time the mothers and children were shut in the customs-shed, hungry and thirsty. They had had nothing to eat since the previous evening. At last the airline people prevailed, and the plane was allowed to go on to Rome. Another long wait, for of course no one was booked on a flight, until a Ghana Airways plane was found which was going to London via Zürich. The whole journey, from D'Aosta Camp to London Airport, took seventeen hours.

Those of us who were left – and this was the great majority of the British civilian population in Cyrenaica, the Americans having been flown out *en masse*, at their government's orders, to Italy and Spain – sank deeper and deeper into depression, trying to get permission to return to our homes, but strictly refused until Saturday and Sunday, June 10th and 11th. To emerge into Libya again after the hermetically-sealed Englishness of life in the camp was a strange and unsettling experience. Armed and helmeted Cydef men were everywhere, many shops were still shut, the streets were unnaturally quiet, and a long curfew was still in force. At the university there was no activity. Istiklal was closed to traffic, assemblies of more than five people were forbidden. Our flat had not been touched, and indeed the only actual looting I heard of was in the British Council director's house in the outskirts of Benghazi, where about £2,500 worth of stuff had been taken. But there was some destruction of property. The director's secretary, who had lived in a flat above part of the British Consulate, had had most of her possessions burned by the mob on June 5th.

The Jews, who had suffered most, were apparently still in the Cydef camp, soon to be evacuated from the country to Italy. Reports came back later that at Benina and Idris airports they had been stripped of all their jewellery and any other valuable property, and that they were living in great poverty and discomfort in a refugee camp near Rome. It was at this time that a government shake-up pushed out Hussein Mazik as prime minister and put in El-Badri, a man who was known to have been a partner of Bedussa, one of the richest Libyan Jews, in several important business enterprises. But this association seemed to do nothing to better the lot of the Jews, nor could the change be seen as a significant shift in policy, for El-Badri wasn't known to be either more militant or more pacific than Mazik, as far as the Palestine Problem was concerned. All that seemed to be felt was that El-Badri was both less honest and less educated, and that Mazik was being shuffled off just to give the impression that changes were being made and that the government was not an immovable mass. Three months later, and El-Badri himself was dismissed, to be replaced by a young Tripolitanian, Bakush.

A week after our release from D'Aosta, the university examinations were resumed, and once more we assembled with our Arab colleagues to invigilate, mark papers, and in general carry on just as we had been on the morning of June 5th. There was a feeling of strain, perhaps, with some of the Egyptians, but none – except for the normal strain of an examination régime – with the students. The curfew continued, but was relaxed a little, and the streets began to fill up with their crowds and to take on their old atmosphere. Only here and there, amid the shuttered wrecks of Jewish shops and the dust now mixed with ash from the burnt-out British and American buildings, did one hear whispers of a mood. Abdulla, an Egyptian painter who had been living in Benghazi for a few months, said that several times he had been greeted when going into shops with such remarks as, 'Here comes one of those Egyptians, the sort that runs away,' and once, 'You Egyptians don't *deserve* to have Nasser.' It was said that some Libyans were actually glad at the news of the Egyptian defeat, seeing it as that and not as a defeat for pan-Arabism. Egypt and Egyptians have never been popular in Libya: a powerful neighbour, with patronizing or condescending attitudes to the 'backward' Libyans, is bound to be resented. But the general mood was one of quiet depression. There had been exuberance, a sudden wild anger and destructiveness, and now nothing but grey uncertainty.

On July 10th, with all my examination work finished, the flat stripped of all its furniture and possessions, my bills paid and my visa in order, I drove down to the docks in Benghazi with the van piled high with suitcases, clothes, and minor antiquarian loot. As it happened, the Vice-Rector was seeing off his uncle on the same boat, and if I had learned one thing in Libya it was how to 'use shoulders', in the Arabic sense – if you know a man with influence, use him. A word with the Vice-Rector, a word passed on to the customs officer, and the van was waved through without inspection and on to the boat. Handshaking all round, a great gust of blustery heat, and the *Citta di Livorno* thumped and grumbled towards Malta and Syracuse, and the long drive north.

List of Publications

F. W. & H. W. Beechey: *Proceedings of the Expedition to Explore the Northern Coast of Africa – from Tripoli Eastwards* (London, 1828).

John Boardman & John Hayes: *Excavations at Tocra 1963–1965: The Archaic Deposits I* (British School of Archaeology at Athens, and Thames & Hudson, 1966).

Giacomo Caputo & Ernesto Vergara Caffarelli: *The Buried City* (Weidenfeld & Nicolson, 1966).

Paolo della Cella: *Narrative of an Expedition from Tripoli in Barbary to the Western Frontier of Egypt,* translated by Anthony Aufrere (London, 1822).

The Economic Development of Libya (Johns Hopkins Press, Baltimore, for the International Bank for Reconstruction and Development, 1960).

E. E. Evans-Pritchard: *The Sanusi of Cyrenaica* (Clarendon Press, Oxford, 1949).

Richard Goodchild: *Benghazi: The Story of a City* (Government Press, Benghazi: latest edition, 1963).

Richard Goodchild: *Cyrene and Apollonia: An Historical Guide* (Antiquities Department, Cyrene: 1959).

D. E. L. Haynes: *Ancient Tripolitania* (Government Press, Tripoli: latest edition, 1963).

R. W. Hill: *A Bibliography of Libya* (Department of Geography, University of Durham, 1959).

Agnes Newton Keith: *Children of Allah* (Michael Joseph, 1966).

Majid Khadduri: *Modern Libya: A Study in Political Development* (Johns Hopkins Press, Baltimore, 1963).

Carl H. Kraeling: *Ptolemais, City of the Libyan Pentapolis* (University of Chicago Press, 1962).

C. B. M. McBurney: *The Stone Age of Northern Africa* (Penguin Books, 1960).

Alan Moorehead: *The Desert War* (Hamish Hamilton, 1965).

Alan Rowe (editor): *Cyrenaican Expeditions of the University of Manchester* (Manchester University Press, two volumes, 1956 and 1959).

Gwyn Williams: *Green Mountain: An Informal Guide to Cyrenaica and its Jebel Akhdar* (Faber, 1963).

Index

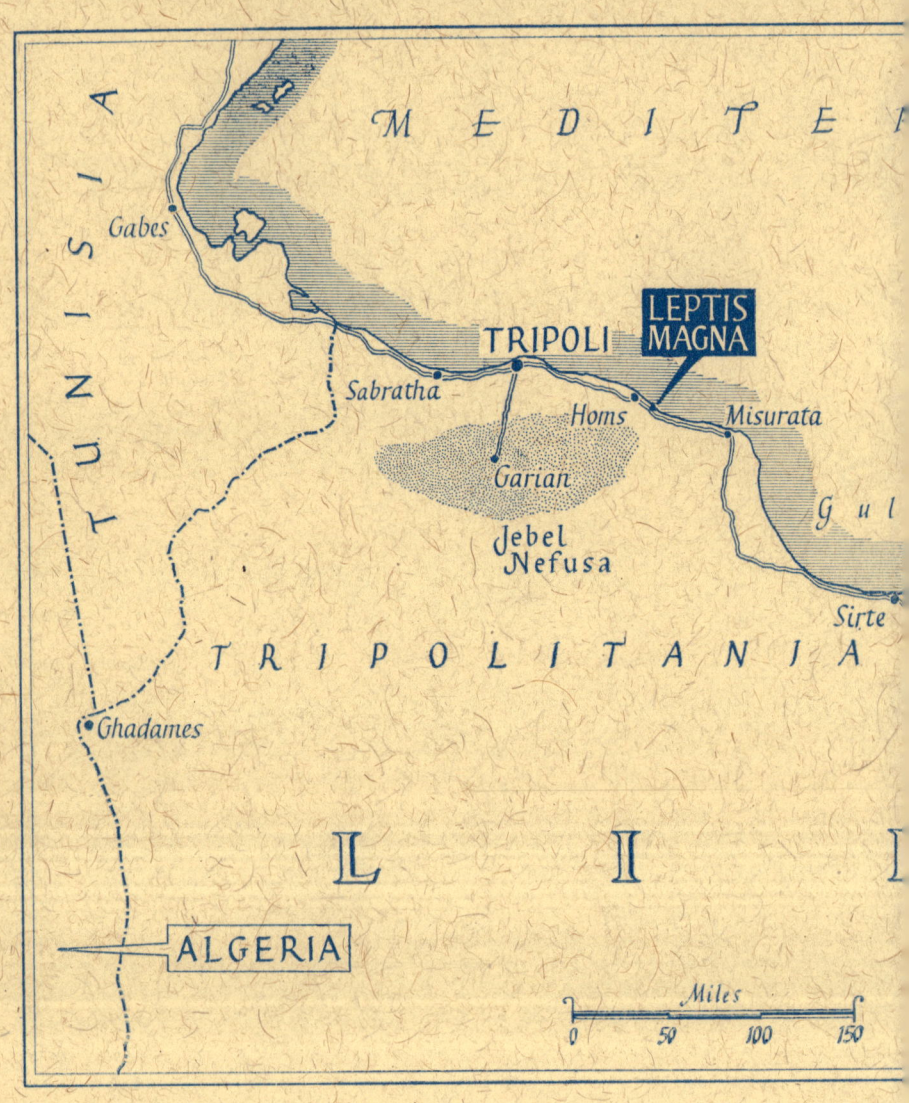

MEDITERR

TUNISIA

Gabes

TRIPOLI

LEPTIS
MAGNA

Sabratha

Homs

Misurata

Garian

Gul

Jebel
Nefusa

Sirte

TRIPOLITANIA

Ghadames

L I   I

ALGERIA

Miles

0   50   100   150